MORE FOUL DEEDS AND SUSPICIOUS DEATHS IN AND AROUND BARNSLEY

TRUE CRIME FROM WHARNCLIFFE

Foul Deeds and Suspicious Deaths Series

Barking, Dagenham & Chadwell Heath
Barnsley
Bath
Bedford
Birmingham
Black Country
Blackburn and Hyndburn
Bolton
Bradford
Brighton
Bristol
Cambridge
Carlisle
Chesterfield
Colchester
Coventry
Croydon
Derby
Dublin
Durham
Ealing
Folkestone and Dover
Grimsby
Guernsey
Guildford
Halifax
Hampstead, Holborn and St Pancras
Huddersfield
Hull

Leeds
Leicester
Lewisham and Deptford
Liverpool
London's East End
London's West End
Manchester
Mansfield
More Foul Deeds Birmingham
More Foul Deeds Chesterfield
More Foul Deeds Wakefield
Newcastle
Newport
Norfolk
Northampton
Nottingham
Oxfordshire
Pontefract and Castleford
Portsmouth
Rotherham
Sheffield
Scunthorpe
Southend-on-Sea
Staffordshire and The Potteries
Stratford and South Warwickshire
Tees
Warwickshire
Wigan
York

OTHER TRUE CRIME BOOKS FROM WHARNCLIFFE

A-Z of Yorkshire Murder
Black Barnsley
Brighton Crime and Vice 1800-2000
Durham Executions
Essex Murders
Executions & Hangings in Newcastle
     and Morpeth
Norfolk Mayhem and Murder

Norwich Murders
Strangeways Hanged
The A-Z of London Murders
Unsolved Murders in Victorian and
     Edwardian London
Unsolved Norfolk Murders
Unsolved Yorkshire Murders
Yorkshire's Murderous Women

Please contact us via any of the methods below for more information or a catalogue.

WHARNCLIFFE BOOKS

47 Church Street – Barnsley – South Yorkshire – S70 2AS
Tel: 01226 734555 – 734222 Fax: 01226 – 734438
E-mail: enquiries@pen-and-sword.co.uk
Website: www.wharncliffebooks.co.uk

More Foul Deeds & Suspicious Deaths in and Around

BARNSLEY

GEOFFREY HOWSE

This book is dedicated to my sister and her husband:
Christine and David Walker

First published in Great Britain in 2009 by
Wharncliffe Local History
an imprint of
Pen & Sword Books Ltd
47 Church Street
Barnsley
South Yorkshire
S70 2AS

Copyright © Geoffrey Howse 2009

ISBN 978-1-84563-086-7

Typeset in 11/13pt Plantin by
Mac Style, Beverley, East Yorkshire

Printed and bound in the UK
by CPI

Pen & Sword Books Ltd incorporates the imprints of Pen & Sword
Aviation, Pen & Sword Maritime, Pen & Sword Military,
Wharncliffe Local History, Pen and Sword Select, Pen and Sword
Military Classics and Leo Cooper.

For a complete list of Pen & Sword titles please contact
PEN & SWORD BOOKS LIMITED
47 Church Street, Barnsley, South Yorkshire, S70 2AS, England
E-mail: enquiries@pen-and-sword.co.uk
Website: www.pen-and-sword.co.uk

Contents

Author's collection

Introduction

I n this my second book concerning True Crime in and around Barnsley I have attempted to build on the popularity of my first volume by selecting a fittingly diverse range of foul deeds from all over the area. Examples range from what is generally considered to be the ultimate crime, that of murder, to somewhat trivial misdemeanours. However, my choice of individual cases serves to illustrate the diversity of sentencing and the changing views towards certain types of crime.

For instance, in 1860, on being found guilty of manslaughter, farmer Isaac Shore was imprisoned for only two months with hard labour, by Mr Justice Hill (see Chapter 8), whereas in 1868, for unlawfully wounding a gamekeeper, bricklayer (and poacher), William Atha, was sent to prison for fifteen months by Mr Justice Lush (see Chapter 5); and in 1933, Hortis Bailey was given six months in prison, by Barnsley magistrates for stealing sixteen fowls (see Chapter 5). It is also worth considering the changing attitude with regard to public morality (see Chapter 14), when one compares what was considered acceptable behaviour in 1952 to what passes for public morality in the England of today, one cannot help but feel appalled. From the huge number of cases I have studied, not only within Barnsley and district, but cases throughout England, I often find myself being bewildered by the extraordinary sentences dished out by both magistrates and judges. During the nineteenth and early twentieth centuries, when many of Barnsley's magistrates were landowners, penalties for game related offences were often disproportionately harsh. It would seem that simply to be poor was regarded by some as tantamount to being a criminal. For the most serious crimes, where the death penalty applied, juries would often convict a man or woman of a lesser offence, rather than see them die at the end of a rope, particularly if they took a liking to the accused person, which they sometimes did. The cut of a man's jib often could be his salvation, or indeed, his downfall. Historically, the administration of justice has been a somewhat arbitrary matter, and in some cases remains so to the present day.

Street betting was a curious crime and one that was often hard to clamp down on, and I have included some examples. This was in the days when off-course betting was a criminal offence. In order to place a bet on a race it was necessary to either be at the race meeting or to have someone place the bet at that actual meeting on your behalf, otherwise to place a bet on a horse race or other sporting event was illegal. When a person acting as an intermediary between the punter and bookmaker, known as a bookmaker's or bookie's runner, was brought to court for taking illegal bets, strict magisterial duties were often disregarded depending on who might be sitting on the Bench, particularly if those sitting were, for example, keen followers of the turf. On seeing the slightest opportunity to acquit they would do so. Whereas a magistrate holding strong religious beliefs, for example, being themselves more likely to be averse to any form of gambling, would often inflict a heavy fine. My paternal grandfather, Isadore Howse, used to operate as a bookie's runner for his great friend Clarrie (Clarence) Evans, who, once off-course betting was legalised, operated from premises in Fitzwilliam Street, Elsecar. My grandfather was never arrested. Hardly surprising, I suppose, when one considers that the local bobby's wife enjoyed a regular bet and her husband habitually pushed her betting slips and wagers through my grandparent's letter box, when he was patrolling his beat, to be retrieved by my grandmother and handed to my grandfather on his return from work, or from his regular watering hole, Elsecar's *Market Hotel*.

Recently I sent a copy of the first volume of my *Foul Deeds and Suspicious Deaths in and Around Barnsley* to a long standing and much loved friend who now lives abroad. I was somewhat nonplussed when my friend commented sometime later, that she had not yet read the book but only glanced through the pages, as she was not familiar with any of the cases. Clearly, the book had not grabbed her attention. One case she had overlooked, with which she was in fact familiar, taking up an

Bookies runner Isadore Howse (left) and Herbert Thickett. Landlord of the Market Hotel, *Elsecar.* Author's collection

entire chapter, involved the perpetrator of possibly the most heinous crime to have been committed within the Barnsley area during the third quarter of the twentieth century, the beast of a man concerned actually lived just a few doors away from her family home at the time he was caught.

My friend Kristin's comments got me thinking. The main reason we are aware of what has occurred in our past is as a direct result of what has actually been recorded. In England, we are fortunate that literacy has enabled the greater portion of the present-day public to read about our history in detail, if they so wish. Many of the more high profile cases are remembered locally, simply by being passed down by word of mouth. But, for the most part, the fact that these events actually happened are simply a matter of record, being included in old court documents, pamphlets, newspapers and magazines. A murder may also remain in the public's consciousness simply because a building or location where the tragedy occurred, is repeatedly being pointed out to newcomers or visitors by local residents. If the fabric of the building remains, the story of the crime continues to pass down through generations.

Few crimes or foul deeds have ever been recorded in published books and all but a tiny portion will only rarely be seen by researchers. To become familiar with a case a person needs to either read about it in books, have it read to them, or have it passed down orally, probably in either a more diluted or possibly a fantastically exaggerated form, depending on who is telling the story. Embroidering the facts often makes a case seem far more interesting that in reality it ever was.

My perplexity at Kristin's comment also brought to mind a favourite film of mine, *Shirley Valentine,* directed by Lewis Gilbert and based on Willy Russells's play of the same title. When, during assembly, Shirley correctly answers the question, 'What was man's most important invention (the answer being 'the wheel')?' the astounded mistress exasperatingly and somewhat grudgingly, expressing the opinion that Shirley must have been told the answer. Shirley, having gleamed that little nugget of knowledge from her father, who had read about it in the *Encyclopaedia Brittanica,* is clearly disgusted as well as disappointed at the response she receives to having correctly answered the question. She cheekily reacts using rhetoric, blurting out in her thick Liverpudlian accent:

How the bloody hell was I supposed to know!

Indeed, how was she?

One of the most important lessons I have learned is that every generation thinks they invented the wheel and nobody but themselves has an opinion worth hearing about or considering. Fortunately, this is not the case and, through the generations, the more enlightened of us attempt to create a more civilized existence for their fellow man.

As I often delve into the Barnsley area's history I am continually being surprised, sometimes even awestruck, at the diversity of crimes and foul deeds I come across, covering a wide timescale and involving people from all classes and virtually every walk of life. In addition to the cases covered here, I have set aside a considerable number of interesting and serious crimes that I hope to include in another volume in the coming years.

I have tried to present a truthful and interesting account of the cases covered here by careful research and thorough cross-referencing of source material but I apologise for any errors or omissions.

Acknowledgements

I am particularly grateful to John D Murray who has assisted me over several years; and to Keith Atack, Vera Atack, Iris Ackroyd, Michael Barber, Susan Barber, Joan Bostwick, Norma Braddick, Robert (Bob) A Dale, Kathleen Dale, Thomas Roscoe Deane (1927–2009), Iris J Deller, Joanna C Murray Deller, Ricky S Deller, Tracy P Deller, Brian Elliott, Doreen Howse, Joy Howse, Kathleen Howse, Dr Hidayat Hussein, Kristin Liptrot, Brenden E McNally, Raymond Mellor-Jones, Pamela Mott, Eleanor Nelder, Stanley Nelder, Anthony Richards, Thawleys Newsagents, Hoyland, Adam R Walker, Anna Walker, Emma C Walker, Ivan P Walker, Suki B Walker, Walker's Newsagents, Hoyland, Clifford Willoughby, Margaret Willoughby, the staff of Barnsley Central Library, Doug Hindmarch, Senior Local Studies Librarian at Sheffield Central Library and the staff at Sheffield Central Library.

Author's collection

CHAPTER 1

A Victorian Miscellany

FOUND GUILTY OF CUTTING LORD WHARNCLIFFE'S UNDERWOOD, CARLTON, 1857

A previous conviction for the same offence had been proved against him...

J S Stanhope, Esquire was in the chair when Samuel Hodgson, resident at Smithies, appeared in the dock at Barnsley courthouse on Wednesday 25 March 1857, charged with cutting underwood in a plantation owned by Lord Wharncliffe, at Carlton. Game watcher Emanuel Cherry told the court that he saw Hodgson on 13 February in Lord Wharncliffe's plantation. Cherry said he observed Hodgson had been engaged in the cutting of about sixty small poles, some of which were nearly two yards long. A previous conviction for the same offence had been proved against him and Hodgson pleaded guilty as charged. He was committed to Wakefield House of Correction for four months.

ROBBERY BY A SERVANT, THURLSTONE, JANUARY 1858

...money had been missing from a particular drawer at various intervals in the past.

On Monday 11 January 1858, Mrs Ann Jubb, who worked in service with her husband, appeared in the dock at Barnsley courthouse before magistrate Thomas Taylor Esquire. Mrs Jubb was charged with stealing 5s 8½d from the counting house of her employer, Mr Thomasson of Thurlstone, on 7 January. Mr Thomasson told the court that money had been missing from a particular drawer at various intervals in the past, without any clue as to who the thief might be. Suspicion had fallen on three possible employees but exactly how the money was stolen was a mystery as the drawer was kept locked. At about eight o'clock in the morning of 7 January, 19*s* 9*d* was placed in the drawer. The money had been especially marked for identification. At nine o'clock, some of the cash was missing. In the interim period Mrs Jubb had been cleaning the counting house. Nobody else could be implicated except Mrs Jubb. She was at once confronted about having taken the missing money and with overwhelming evidence against her immediately admitted that she was the culprit. The mystery of how Mrs Jubb obtained entry to the drawer was cleared up by her husband who produced a key belonging to his wife that fitted the drawer. Mr Thomasson said he could find no excuse for Mrs Jubb having robbed him of money as both she and her husband were paid good wages and they had no family to support. Despite this, he evidently felt somewhat compassionate towards his servant as he declined to press the case to the full extent the law permitted. Mrs Jubb got off lightly when she was sentenced to a month with hard labour at Wakefield House of Correction.

VIOLENT ASSAULT ON A CONSTABLE, WOMBWELL, FEBRUARY 1858

…the constable had his clothes almost torn from his back.

On Friday 19 February 1858, police constable Hey was on patrol in Wombwell when he was approached by a woman who said that a neighbour, William Haley, was killing his wife. Constable Hey went to Haley's house nearby, and, as he approached, Haley came out with a poker in his hand and threatened to 'cut him in two' if he entered. The constable tried to reason with Haley but Haley seized hold of him and both fell to the ground. A long struggle ensued during which the constable had his clothes almost torn from his back, as well as having one of his fingers bitten very badly. On Wednesday 24

February 1858, William Haley was brought up before magistrates at Barnsley courthouse, charged with committing an aggravated assault against constable Hey. Several witnesses were called who corroborated constable Hey's statement. Superintendent Burke said, 'The charge against Haley is laid under the Constabulary Act, by which the Bench has the power to inflict a penalty of £20 or in default to commit the defendant for six months. This is a very serious offence and I must ask the magistrates to make an example of this man.' In the mid-Victorian period, magistrates, particularly high-born ones, did not take kindly to being told what they must do. Their priorities, with regard to dishing out justice, was jealously guarded. Some dealt harshly with what today we would regard as relatively petty offences; whereas, more serious offences, sometimes received relatively light sentences. The Bench, consisting of Thomas Taylor, Esquire, Godfrey Wentworth, Esquire and J B Stanhope, Esquire, fined Haley £5, or in default to be kept to hard labour for three months at Wakefield House of Correction. That same morning, the Bench had given a man a fine of £2 for merely being caught with a gun in a wood (see Chapter 5). Both these fines were of a considerably high value by the standards of the day, £2 representing more than two weeks' wages for the average working man.

FINED FOR ASSAULTING A FELLOW SERVANT AT WORTLEY HALL, 1859

...seized her by the hair pulling on it so hard that Mary was forced backwards onto the floor

The magistrates sitting on the Bench at Barnsley courthouse on Wednesday 26 January 1859 were Godfrey Wentworth, Esquire, Thomas Taylor, Esquire and W S Stanhope, Esquire. The first case to come up before them was an assault. Jane Jones, one of Lord and Lady Wharncliffe's servants at Wortley Hall, was charged with having assaulted fellow servant, Mary Jones, on 14 January. The court heard that although the women bore the same surname they were not related. Mr Hamer appeared for the complainant and Mr Tyas for the defendant. On Friday 14 January, Mary Jones was sitting down in a room in the hall making spells with which to light the hall's many fires. Jane Jones came into the room carrying a coal scuttle, full of coals. She put the scuttle down on Mary's dress, and carried on about her business in that room as if nothing untoward had happened. When Mary realised what Jane had done she remarked upon it. Jane came over to apparently leave the room, picked up the scuttle and tipped the coals over Mary, then seized her by the hair pulling on it so hard that Mary was forced backwards onto the floor, where Jane knelt on her chest and attempted to throttle her. Whereupon Mary called out:

Murder, murder, murder!

Some other servants quickly came to her assistance. Anne Jones was pulled off Mary and stood nearby in an agitated state. When she had come to her senses, Mary got up off the floor and was immediately struck twice with a broom by Jane. She was about to strike her a third blow when another servant, Louisa Scaife, intervened and wrestled the broom from her. Mr Tyas asked Mary if she had given the defendant any reason for her actions. Mary said she had not. Louisa Scaife was

Wortley Hall. Author's collection

called as a witness. She said she had heard someone call murder three times and found the two girls with their hair pulled down and Mary Jones's face black with coal dirt. She said she saw the defendant strike Mary twice with a broom but wrestled it off her, as she was about to strike a third blow. Mary Millett provided similar evidence. Found guilty as charged, Jane Jones was ordered to pay a fine of 5s and expenses.

VIOLENT ASSAULT ON A POLICE OFFICER, WORSBROUGH DALE, 1861

He knows us; let's kill the bugger.

On the night of Monday 1 April 1861, Police Constable James Ackroyd Morley was on duty in Worsbrough Dale, near the *Mason's Arms*, kept by Mr Pickles. A man named James Scaife came up to the officer and asked him for a light. As Constable Morley turned on his lamp, he noticed some men he recognised as Thomas Pashley, James McQuillan, Aaron Kilner and Ambrose Haigh, along with some others, standing at the corner of the street. As Constable Morley was about to give Scaife a Lucifer match, Pashley ran at the constable and knocked him down. The constable got up and seized Pashley, whereupon Kilner came over and he and Scaife started kicking Constable Morley, getting him to the ground while adding punches to the kicks. Pashley then called out:

He knows us; lets kill the bugger.

Having said that, Pashley jumped with both feet on the constable's side, at which point Constable Morley called out in a loud voice:

Murder!

This prompted all the men to run away. Constable Morley was left bleeding from the eyes, nose and mouth. As well as several cuts, he received some serious bruising to the head, face and shoulder, and a broken rib. The injured constable was attended to by surgeon, Mr Wainwright. Scaife, Pashley, Kilner, McQuillan and Haigh were subsequently rounded up, arrested and charged with assault.

Having been remanded twice, the prisoners appeared in the dock at Barnsley courthouse on Wednesday 17 April, before Thomas Taylor, Esquire and Colonel Daly. Mr Hamer prosecuted and Mr Whitfield, of Rotherham appeared for the prisoners. Mr Hamer asked the magistrates to discharge Ambrose Haigh, as there was no evidence against him but he did propose to call Haigh as a witness.

Constable Morley described the attack and told the court that in addition to the injuries he had received, his attackers had also taken his hat and cape, torn his trousers and broken his lamp to pieces. The hat was returned to his house the following day. It had been badly crushed. The cape was also returned to him. It had been found some distance from the scene of the attack. Constable Morley added that since the attack he had been off duty and remained under the care of Mr Wainwright.

A present-day view of the Mason's Arms, *Worsbrough Dale.* Brian Elliott collection

Ambrose Haigh said on the night of the attack he was in company with the four prisoners. He saw the constable knocked down but could not say who did it, as the night was so very dark. He also heard someone kicking the constable. He left as quickly as possible with Scaife, as he did not wish to get involved in the affray. The following morning, he had met with the four prisoners, when Pashley had admitted knocking the constable down and Kilner and McQuillan to striking and kicking him. The surgeon, Mr Wainwright, confirmed the injuries Constable Morley had received in the attack.

Mr Hamer asked the Bench to commit the prisoners to the next sessions for trial. The Bench, however, disregarded this request, following Mr Whitfield's address in mitigation of the offences, which he said were committed while the men were in high spirits and that they were very contrite and sincerely sorry for their deplorable behaviour. After a short discussion, a decision was made that the case should be dealt with summarily. The magistrates fined Pashley £2, Kilner £1, and Scaife and McQuillan 5s each, plus expenses in each case, or in default to be committed to Wakefield House of Correction for two months.

TO BE FOREWARNED IS TO BE FOREARMED. HIGHWAY ROBBERY, GAWBER, 1862

...Donkin had fast hold of the old man's throat, and Sowden was engaged in ransacking the basket.

In April 1862, the network of criminal intelligence that existed in and around Barnsley, through the usual copper's narks and other sources was to provide police with a major coup. Police Superintendent Greenhalgh received information concerning a robbery planned for Saturday 5 April. It concerned a wage snatch that was to take place between Barnsley and Gawber. Two of the names mentioned were known to police: William Donkin and John Hewitt. Another man, Thompson Sowden was also to be involved.

Charles Smith, aged seventy-eight, had been in the employ of Messrs Sturges, Paley, and Co for forty years. They were the proprietors of the New Gawber Colliery. One of his regular duties required him to go once a fortnight to Barnsley to obtain small change for the purpose of paying the miners. On Saturday 5 April, Mr Smith went to Barnsley as usual, where he obtained £20 (the equivalent of over £12,400 today) in silver from various tradesmen, 6s of which he changed into copper. He left Barnsley between twelve and one o'clock having purchased some groceries, which he placed into a basket with the bags of money. He proceeded on his usual route, which took him past a railway bridge by which he sat down to rest for a few minutes. While he was sitting there, three men walked by, one of which he later recognised as William Donkin. Soon afterwards, Mr Smith got up and continued on his journey homewards towards the colliery. He turned down a field to the left of the road and carried on walking to a footbridge by the Honey Well. Unbeknown to Mr Smith, Superintendent Greenhalgh had a policeman concealed at various points on the route taken by the old man, in case he was attacked. Several men were positioned in the immediate vicinity of Honeywell Lane, two waited behind some haystacks and two were near the footbridge. Superintendent Greenhalgh had also concealed himself behind a haystack, from where he had a good view.

From his vantage point, the Superintendent saw Donkin and Sowden seize Mr Smith and throw him down. He immediately fired a pistol to alert his men. Four of them rushed up to the scene of the robbery. Donkin and Sowden had the old man laid on the ground and had stuffed a handkerchief into his mouth. The basket Mr Smith had been carrying was broken open and the bags of money strewn upon the ground. Donkin and Sowden were apprehended after a short struggle. Donkin was found to have the bag containing 6s in copper in his pocket. Hewitt, who was standing watch about twenty-five yards away was also taken into custody. The three men were brought up before magistrates at Barnsley Courthouse, on Monday 7 April, where they were committed to appear at the next assizes.

On Wednesday 16 July, John Hewitt, William Donkin and Thompson Sowden appeared before Mr Justice Mellor at the Yorkshire Summer Assizes. Mr Maule and Mr Hannay prosecuted. Mr Foster defended Hewitt; Mr Vernon Blackburn defended Donkin and Sowden. Mr Hindle, surveyor from Barnsley, produced a plan showing the locality where the robbery took place. The victim of the robbery, Charles Smith, after outlining the events of the earlier part of his day, described how he had been attacked and robbed. He described the route he had taken up until he had reached the end of the long field, after which he went towards the footbridge crossing near the Honey Well. As he approached he saw one of the men who had passed him earlier standing on the bridge. There was a stile nearby and as he neared it he noticed another man standing close by. This man seized hold of him and threw him down. A handkerchief was stuffed in his face and another man came up. He recognised him as Donkin. Shortly after that the police arrived and he got up off the ground and began to look after his money, which had been scattered about.

Superintendent Greenhalgh said he was posted near some haystacks. At about five minutes to one, on 5 April, he saw the three prisoners together in company. He also observed them follow Mr Smith and throw him down. Superintendent Greenhalgh said, 'I then fired the pistol and called upon Sykes to follow me. When I got up to them I saw Brannagan and Lawes seize Donkin and Sowden, who were close by the old man they were robbing. I found £18 12s in silver, emptied out of the basket on the ground.'

Inspector George Sykes said when the pistol was fired he ran with the superintendent in the direction of Honey Well. He noticed Hewitt about twenty-five yards from Mr Smith was struggling with the other two prisoners. He noticed the other officers take Donkin and Sowden into custody. When he got up to them he spoke to Sowden whose face was covered with blood. Sowden asked him to wipe it, which the inspector did. Sergeant Thomas Brannagan noticed Sowden and Donkin seize the old man, and he then ran up to the spot, where he found Donkin had fast hold of the old man's throat, and Sowden was engaged in ransacking the basket. He saw the two men apprehended amidst a scuffle, and saw Hewitt coming towards the scene before he quickly turned round and made off in the opposite direction.

Mr Foster, in Hewitt's defence, contended that there was no evidence against his client. He was merely taking a walk in the locality, and happened to be near where the robbery occurred, he was supposed to be a scout, and had consequently been charged with participation in the crime, with which the two other men were charged. Mr Blackburn recommended that his client's Dodkin and Sowden be shown mercy. He said that no great degree of violence had been used, and even this might have been prevented if the police had exercised due discretion. They had some knowledge of the affair, and they ought rather to have prevented the robbery, than have allowed the old man to be knocked down and ill used.

Mr Justice Mellor said in answer to Mr Blackburn's comments:

> *I do not know that in this case the conduct of the police was at all censurable. The offence was a most audacious one and I will visit it with a severe punishment.*

All three prisoners were given a sentence of four years' penal servitude.

NEGLECT OF A FAMILY, BARNSLEY, 1863

...the appalling conduct of her husband, had prompted the Guardians to press for a conviction.

Pit labourer Henry Jackson appeared at Barnsley courthouse on Monday 11 May 1863, before Thomas Taylor, Esquire, charged with allowing his wife and family to become chargeable to the Barnsley Union. The circumstances that had brought the unfortunate woman and her children to the workhouse and the appalling conduct of her husband, had prompted the Guardians to press for a conviction. The court heard that sometime at the beginning of April, whilst his wife was confined to her bed through sickness, Jackson had departed from Barnsley in the company of a female, leaving his wife and children destitute. Urgent steps were taken to ascertain his whereabouts and a letter was sent to him.

Meanwhile, on 15 April, Mrs Jackson and her children had obtained relief at the workhouse. Shortly afterwards, her husband's reply arrived. He said that the woman with whom he was cohabiting was heavily pregnant and was shortly to be confined. He went on to say he would send some money to his wife as soon as he could afford it. This news adversely affected Mrs Jackson's health and she died within a few days. Henry Jackson stood in the box as he was berated by the Bench for what they considered to be his disgraceful conduct. He was committed to Wakefield House of Correction for one month with hard labour.

WIFE ASSAULT, DARTON, 1864

...he immediately began to beat her and afterwards turned her out of the house.

On Wednesday 10 August 1864, Henry Hobson was in the dock at Barnsley courthouse, before Walter S Stanhope, Esquire and the Rev Henry Bowen Cooke, charged with assaulting his wife Hannah, at Darton on 12 July. The Hobsons had been married for three years. The marriage did not appear to have been a happy one, as during the relatively short period since the wedding the couple had parted no fewer than thirteen times. On Tuesday 12 July, Hobson asked his wife to draw some porter and to bring it to him in bed. She did as he requested and having done so, he immediately began to beat her and afterwards turned her out of the house. His wife having left the house, Hobson then handed the porter to his neighbours and they drank until the entire barrel was empty. After the Bench discussed the matter of the assault with the Hobsons, the charge was not proceeded with as the couple decided to separate. Henry Hobson agreed to pay 3s 6d a week for his wife's maintenance and to pay the court costs.

OBTAINING MONEY BY FALSE PRETENCES, PENISTONE, JANUARY 1865

...a man who had twice before obtained money from him, as he had later discovered, by making false statements.

Magistrate T E Taylor, Esquire, was no doubt surprised to discover his own name on a list of subscribers, which also included Lord Wharncliffe, written in a book given in evidence and found, following his arrest, upon the prisoner in the dock at Barnsley courthouse on Monday 23 January 1865. John William Smith was charged with obtaining money by false pretences at Penistone on 19 January. On that day, Smith paid a visit to the Rev W G Turnbull in Penistone. Mr Turnbull saw Smith approaching the house from his study window and immediately recognised him as a man who had twice before obtained money from him, as he had later discovered, by making false statements. Mr Turnbull instructed his servant to show Smith into an adjoining room and meanwhile sent for a police officer. Having done so Mr Turnbull went to see Smith who immediately embarked on a long rambling tale of woe. He said he was a parishioner who found himself in greatly reduced circumstances due to the misconduct of an uncle. In order to obtain money from Mr Turnbull, Smith told him that he was a hawker by trade and he was a little short of the sum he needed to purchase a horse and cart to enable him to resume trading. He said that Mr Rolling had given him 2s 6d and Mr Tomason 3s 6d. In order to buy himself a little time to enable a police officer to arrive, Mr Turnbull gave Smith 1s. Shortly afterwards Smith was arrested and the aforementioned book found on his person in which was a list of names and subscriptions amounting to almost £11. The charge against Smith having been proven, Mr Taylor sentenced him to three months at Wakefield House of Correction.

A TASTE FOR HOT VEGETABLES, HOYLAND NETHER AND ELSECAR, AUGUST 1865

...found asleep in a field with his pockets full of onions...

When faced with overwhelming evidence against a prisoner in the dock at Barnsley courthouse, on Monday 14 August 1865, Rev H B Shaw held no reservations when he handed down a stiff sentence to the miscreant. The court heard that in the early hours of Friday 4 August William Foy was spotted by Charles Hawke leaving his garden in Hoyland Nether carrying a sack. Mr Hawke had a good look round and shortly afterwards gave information to the police concerning the theft of vegetables from his garden and the discovery of a quantity of wine, spirits and beer bottles there. Foy was apprehended later that day, having been found asleep in a field with his pockets full of onions, clearly suffering from the after effects of strong drink. As well as the onions, Foy had also stolen some cabbages and savoys and a quantity of smaller vegetables. Evidence was given to show that a few hours earlier than Mr Hawke had seen Foy in his garden, a window at premises kept by Mr W Hodgson, the *New Inn*, Elsecar, had been broken and bottles of wine, spirits and beer stolen. Some of the stolen items were identified as the empty bottles found in Mr Hawke's garden. Foy was committed to Wakefield House of Correction for three months.

SHOPKEEPER ASSAULTS BEERHOUSE KEEPER, ELSECAR, 1866

...kicked him in the face, knocking a tooth out and loosening three others.

On Wednesday 15 August 1866, shopkeeper Henry Stebbing appeared before magistrates at Barnsley courthouse, charged with assault. The Bench were told that in the early hours of 3 August Stebbing was in the company of beerhouse keeper, Joseph Parkin, at the *Fitzwilliam Arms*, Elsecar. They were

A present day view of the Fitzwilliam Arms, *Elsecar, viewed from Wilkinson Road. Until the 1960's the area to the left of the public house in Hill Street (formerly Stubbin) was tightly packed with buildings, which included two former public houses, several shops and houses, including two terraces, which traversed the hillside. The spire of Holy Trinity Church in the village of Wentworth can be seen on the horizon* The author

playing dominoes with others, with drinks as prizes for the winning players. Parkin won a particular game, which had a prize of porter and whisky. However, an argument ensued when Stebbing alleged that Parkin had cheated him, to which allegation Parkin replied that Stebbing was a fool, Stebbing struck Parkin and knocked him down and, while he was on the ground, kicked him in the face, knocking a tooth out and loosening three others. Stebbing denied kicking Parkin but admitted that he had struck him through great provocation. The Bench imposed a fine of 1*s.* and expenses.

ASSAULT AT HOYLANDSWAINE, 1867

...he was struck on the head with a poker.

On Monday 9 December 1867, four members of the same family stood in the dock at Barnsley courthouse, charged with assault, before the Rev H B Cooke, the Hon F S Wortley, R C

Clarke, Esquire and T F C Vernon Wentworth, Esquire. The brothers James and Joseph Clarkson, Elizabeth Clarkson and Robert Clarkson (wife and son of Joseph Clarkson), were charged with assaulting Elisha Swainson, at Hoylandswaine on 10 November. Mr Swainson occupied a cottage with his mother, renting it from Mr John Halliwell of Dodworth. The Clarksons rented a stable from the same landlord. There had been an ongoing dispute about the Clarksons taking water for their horses from a pump, which was said to be for the common use of the cottage properties. When Mr Swainson confronted the Clarksons about them taking water, he was struck on the head with a poker. The landlord was called and the Clarksons were told that the pump was only to be used by them when there was more water available than the tenants required. The Bench imposed a fine of 1s each on the Clarksons.

ATTEMPTED MURDER, THURGOLAND, 1868

...he again got the knife and stabbed himself in the throat.

On Wednesday 15 January 1868, James Esmond appeared at Barnsley courthouse, before W S Stanhope, Esquire and the Rev H B Cooke, charged under the Aggravated Assault Act, with attempting to cut his wife's throat at Thurgoland. Mrs Esmond was heavily pregnant and close to her confinement. Her husband, James, worked at the Silkstone Common Coke Works. On the evening of Friday 10 January, his wife saw him sharpening a clasp knife. When she asked him if he was going to kill them all, he replied, 'No, I will not hurt an hair of your heads, but we shall all be angels before morning.' The next day, he again got the knife and stabbed himself in the throat. Mrs Esmond took hold of her husband's hand, in an attempt to prevent him inflicting further damage to himself, but he turned round and cut her twice in the throat. She struggled and got away from him to the house of a neighbour, Mrs Lawson, who took care of her. The police were sent for and James Esmond was arrested. He pleaded guilty as charged but in mitigation said, 'I have been drinking for some time, and have got right weak.' Despite the relative seriousness of this case, the Bench decided to deal with it summarily. They committed Esmond to Wakefield House of Correction for six months. At the completion of this sentence, the prisoner was further ordered to provide sureties to keep the peace for six months.

GAROTTE ROBBERY AT BARNSLEY, 1871

… took half a sovereign and a florin from his right-hand pocket.

Twenty-year-old collier Walter Kaye and eighteen-year-old labourer Richard Sills appeared at Leeds Spring Assizes on Wednesday 29 March 1871, charged with assaulting and robbing Henry Fisher, at Barnsley on 19 March. Mr Atkinson appeared for the prosecution. Mr Wheelhouse represented both prisoners. Outlining the case for the prosecution, Mr Atkinson said that, late on the night of 19 March, Henry Fisher left the *Trafalgar Inn*, where he had been drinking, and set off home. When he reached Newlands he was attacked by the prisoners, both of whom were well known to him. While one of his assailants throttled him, the other took half a sovereign and a florin from his right-hand pocket. When Fisher called out 'Murder,' his cries were heard by two policemen, who ran to his aid, catching the two prisoners in the act. In the prisoners' defence, Mr Wheelhouse maintained that the incident was nothing more than a case of larking about and horseplay, which formed part and parcel of a collier's life. Both Kaye and Sills were found guilty and sentenced to twelve months' imprisonment.

EXTRAORDINARY CONFESSION TO A HOYLAND MURDER AT BIRMINGHAM, 1879

… confessed to murdering a young woman, named Sarah Cross, nine or ten years previously, at Hoyland Nether.

During the first week of June 1879, several newspapers reported that a thirty-eight-year-old boilermaker, named

Joseph Dewhirst, had appeared at Birmingham Police Court on Monday 3 June, as a result of his own confession, on a charge of wilful murder. Newspapers throughout the West Riding described how Dewhirst had confessed to murdering a young woman, named Sarah Cross, nine or ten years previously, at Hoyland Nether.

A full transcript of Dewhirst's confession was published in newspapers on the day following his appearance in court:

About nine years ago, I think in July, I murdered a woman named Sarah Cross aged about 19 years, with whom I kept company. I murdered her in Loy Meadows, near Hoyland, between Stubbin and Elsecar, Yorkshire. I shot her with a pistol, which I afterwards threw into Wentworth reservoir. At the time I murdered her I worked for George Dawes, Elsecar Ironworks, Elsecar. I then lived at Wood's Row, Hoyland, with my mother. Sarah Cross, lived at a village called Milton, near Hoyland. I murdered her because I caught her with a man named William Pepper, a puddler living at Sebasotpole [sic], Hoyland. After I murdered Sarah Cross, I went straight away to Sheffield, and then to Swindon, where I robbed a man named Joseph Crump of a suit of clothes to disguise myself with. I then returned to Sheffield, then into North Staffordshire, then to Birmingham. The hour I shot Sarah Cross was eight o'clock p.m. My mother with whom I lived when I committed the murder, now lives at 50 Bertingham-street, Occupation-road, Sheffield. I also broke into a chapel, near Worcester-street, Birmingham. About two years ago I also robbed Ned Oakley, with whom I lodged at Tunstall; we both worked at the Old Works, Tunstall.

It was later discovered that Dewhirst had made up the street name where he said his mother had lived. Following his revelations, reporters were despatched to the Hoyland area, with a remit to supply their respective newspapers with sufficiently lurid information to provide them with sensational headlines. Further revelations unfolded as the week progressed, prompting the *Barnsley Chronicle* to report, on Saturday 7 June:

Our Sheffield Contemporaries lost no time in despatching their SPECIAL COMMISSIONERS TO THE SCENE OF THE MURDER, each being furnished with a Carte Blanche *to manufacture an unlimited supply of genuine murder copy, garnished with the usual sensational head-lines of a kind similar to those which were in such requisition during the reign of the late lamented saint and martyr, Charles Peace.*

However, nowhere in Hoyland itself could any clue be obtained to lead reporters to either verify or contradict the information contained in Dewhirst's confession. It was to be a local police officer who was, with just a small amount of investigation, to bring some clarity in the search for the murder victim. In a somewhat tongue-in-cheek account the *Barnsley Chronicle* reported how one particular Sheffield reporter had gone to see the local Police Sergeant at Elsecar:

…At last the happy idea seems to have struck him that he might do worse than see the village policeman, and accordingly he proceeded to interview Sergt. Glover., whom after the fashion of the genuine 'liner' he designate 'a very intelligent officer,' a finding which we are quite happy to endorse. Glover seemed to have an idea and acted upon that idea, he marched his interviewer off to 'the foot of a cliff termed Sebastapole, which is said to have obtained its cognomen from the fact that its inhabitants are always fighting. It seems to be a sort of craggy peninsular of Hoyland, abounding in dirt and second rate cottages. It may be 'a peninsular' but it is scarcely like other peninsulas, for so far from it being nearly, or even partly surrounded with water, we have always been given to understand that there is rather a scarcity of that liquid in this classic region. However, on this 'peninsula' he found a Mrs King, and her daughter, who is about 28 years of age, and on inquiry the latter turned out to be the identical lady who was murdered nine years ago!

Sergeant Glover sent his report to Superintendent Sykes at the West Riding Constabluary headquarters at Barnsley, it read:

Police Office, Elsecar, June 3rd 1879.

Joseph Dewhirst's confession of the murder of Sarah Cross.

Sir, – I beg most respectfully to report to you that I have seen in to-day's Sheffield Telegraph *a report respecting the above named man confessing to the murder of the above named woman, 9 or 10 years ago, at Hoyland, in this section. Acting on the newspaper report I have made enquiry into the case, and have found that a man of that name did court Sarah Cross about that time. I have seen the woman – she is married and lives in Hoyland with William Pepper – and admitted to me to have been courted by the man, and they differed respecting something in courtship, and when he was going away she saw him in the fields between Milton and Hoyland. He told her then he was going away, and would not come back any more, and she hoped God would go with him and keep him away from here. The last she heard of him, some five or six years ago, he was in Birmingham, but said he had enlisted in the Marines. I have no doubt that this will be the same man and woman as she stated these facts to be so frankly and, expecting a report from you to make enquiry. I thought I was only doing my duty to let you know as soon as possible. I am, sir,*

Your most obdt. Servant,
Robt. Glover, Sergt. 128

To
Mr Supt. Sykes,
W. R. C., Barnsley.

At the conclusion of its own report, the *Barnsley Chronicle* commented:

It is doubtless rather provoking to find that the victim will not plead guilty to having been murdered at any period within the last nine or ten years. At any rate she is to all appearances alive and well …

The former Miss Cross, now Mrs Pepper, expressed the desire never to see her former suitor again. It was generally assumed that Dewhirst had made his false confession, in an attempt to secure a free ride back to Yorkshire.

TANKERSLEY GAMBLERS FINED, 1884

...playing at pitch-and-toss at Westwood Bottom.

The mayor (Alderman Tyas), F H Taylor, Esquire and C Harvey, Esquire, were on the Bench at Barnsley West Riding Court, on the last Monday of February 1884, when a group of men from Tankersley were brought up charged with gambling there on 17 February. Samuel Marshall, Thomas Jones, Thomas Bentley and A Walker, all pleaded guilty. Police Constable Smith said that he and Police Constable Wood saw the defendants, and others (five of whom had already been dealt with on 18 February), playing at pitch-and-toss (a gambling game where the player who manages to throw a coin closest to a mark gets to toss all the coins, winning those that land head up) at Westwood Bottom. Marshall, the ringleader, was fined 20*s.*, the other men were fined 10*s.* each and costs.

MINER GETS SIX MONTHS WITH HARD LABOUR FOR STEALING SOAP, BARNSLEY, 1892

...Hirst was apprehended in the warehouse, although not without a struggle.

On Thursday 28 July 1890, Albert Hirst, a thirty-nine-year-old miner, was indicted at Leeds Assizes for breaking into a warehouse at Barnsley on 3 July and stealing 2lbs of soap valued at 4d., the property of Abel Goldthorpe. Mr Alexander, appearing for the prosecution, said that Mr Goldthorpe kept a grocery shop in Sheffield Road, and attached to his property was a small outhouse, which he used as a warehouse. In the early hours of 3 July, between two and three o'clock, Mr Goldthorpe heard a noise in the yard. When he looked out of his window, he saw the prisoner interfering with his warehouse door. Mr Goldthorpe quickly dressed and went downstairs and into the street to search for a policeman. Mr Goldthorpe soon found Sergeant Plowright, who was on patrol nearby. The sergeant returned with Mr Goldthorpe to his premises and Hirst was apprehended in the warehouse, although not without a struggle. When Hirst was searched, 2lbs of soap was found on his person. The defence claimed that on the evening preceding Hirst's arrest, his wife was the worse for drink. Hirst had several glasses of beer himself and an argument ensued between husband and wife, which resulted in Hirst deciding to sleep in Mr Goldthorpe's yard. A guilty verdict was pronounced. As Hirst had several other convictions against him, he was sentenced to six months' imprisonment with hard labour.

TAILOR'S TRAVELLER SENT TO PRISON FOR EMBEZZLEMENT, BARNSLEY, 1892

When I employed him I knew that he had been convicted of felony, but he asked me to give him another chance to redeem his character and I did so.

On a Monday in February 1893, a young Barnsley man, Robert Marshall Christie, a tailor's traveller, was brought up on remand before Barnsley magistrates charged with having embezzled on 13 June 1892 £1 12s. and varying amounts on other dates, from his employer, Mr Daniel Payne, tailor and draper, of Pontefract Road, Barnsley. The magistrate's clerk told the court that a warrant was granted for the defendant's apprehension, in August 1892. Mr J Carrington, prosecuting said that the prisoner had been a traveller for Mr Payne up until the previous July. His duties included taking out parcels of goods to customers throughout Barnsley and district on a day to day basis and afterwards to collect money for these goods, paid by the customer in instalments and to return to his employer's premises each evening and hand the money over to him. Since the warrant had been issued, Mr Payne had gone through his books and ascertained that a sum of money totalling about £50 was missing, due to the felonious conduct of his former employee. Mr Carrington said that he intended to go into five items totalling £1 12*s.* for the purposes of the case and the evidence would show that the prisoner had been given five sums of money making up that total, had issued receipts to customers for the money he had received from them, and that he had not given this money over to his employer. Witnesses were called in support of the prosecution's case. George Livesley, a mechanic, of Canal Street, Barnsley, Emma Fisher, wife of Frank Fisher, also of Canal Street and Mary Ann Freeman, wife of Albert Freeman, hay and straw dealer of Graham's Orchard, Barnsley, gave evidence to the effect that they had all made purchases of shirting, cashmere and other items, in April, May and June 1892, and to having on account of those goods made payments to the prisoner, for which he had issued them with receipts. Mr Payne had not received any money on account of those debts and his ledger was produced in evidence. The prisoner then cross-examined his former employer:

Christie: *Where are the pay-sheets that I made up at night?*
Mr Payne: *You were supposed to make them out, but some of them*
                 are missing. I have not [got] *them with me, they are at*
                 home.
Bench: *The witness said the prisoner neglected to make some of*
                 the pay-sheets out.
Christie: *Have you any debts of mine?*
Mr Payne: *He handed me as security a bogus book of debts, which*
                 alleged that £30 or £40 was due to him.
Christie: *Did you agree to pay me 12*s. *in the £ for the debts?*
Mr Payne: *For all the* bone fide *debts recorded in the book.*
Christie: *For all the debts; Do you think I would sell debts worth*
                 *20*s. *in the £ for 12*s.*?*

When questioned by the Bench, Mr Payne said he could not say whether some traveller of his had received amounts that were in the book:

Christie: *You took me into your employ with a shilling for each*
                 new customer and ten per cent on the collections?

Mr Payne: (Addressing the Bench) *No; I employed him at a pound a week and a shilling a day for expenses besides railway fare; no shilling per new customer.*

Christie: *Did you say your two sons were not agreeable for you to employ me?*

Mr Payne: *That is what they were not.*

Christie: *Did you pay me for the last week that I showed up?*

Mr Payne: *No; because you didn't show up.* (laughter)

Christie: *Did I go to Wombwell with your traveller?*

Mr Payne: *I don't know; but you ran away and left him.*

Mr Payne was re-examined at the Bench's request. During the questioning Mr Payne said:

> *When I employed him I knew that he had been convicted of felony, but he asked me to give him another chance to redeem his character and I did so.*

A witness was called for the defence. Mary Alice Brierley, wife of Thomas Brierley, of Nelson Street, Barnsley, said that in April 1892 she had bought goods from the defendant to the value of 16s. and 10s. 6d. She had been repaying the money to the prisoner in instalments and she had since paid the sum of 3s. to a man named Johnson who was now travelling for Mr Payne.

Christie was asked if he would prefer to be tried at the Assizes, to which question he initially answered in the affirmative. However, after a few moments he had changed his mind and requested that the case should be proceeded with. The Bench, chaired by C Brady, Esquire, also consisted of H Pigott, Esquire, T Dymond, Esquire and J Mitchell Esquire. Mr Brady told Christie:

> *… Of course in a case of this kind the Bench cannot keep out of sight the fact that you have been convicted several times before of similar offences, you having on one occasion been sentenced to six months.*

Mr Brady went on to say that, having considered the evidence, the Bench had formed the opinion that the case had been fully proved. Christie was sentenced to three months' imprisonment.

Author's collection

CHAPTER 2

An Edwardian Assortment

MINER STABBED WITH POCKET KNIFE, WOMBWELL, FEBRUARY 1901

...dealing him a violent blow on the chest, the strength of which knocked him to the ground.

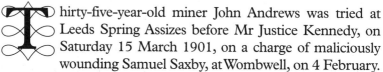hirty-five-year-old miner John Andrews was tried at Leeds Spring Assizes before Mr Justice Kennedy, on Saturday 15 March 1901, on a charge of maliciously wounding Samuel Saxby, at Wombwell, on 4 February.
Mr Alexander, prosecuting, said that the charge against Andrews was a serious one because of the alleged use of a knife. Both Andrews and Saxby were miners. On the day of the incident both men had been freely partaking of alcohol at a working men's club, where they played various games together and ultimately argued over a game of draughts. Andrews was heard to threaten Saxby and, on leaving the club, he attacked him in Garr Street, dealing him a violent blow on the chest, the strength of which knocked him to the ground. When on the witness stand Saxby said that he saw a white-shafted knife in the prisoner's hand. The cut penetrated his clothing, which was several layers thick and caused a wound that bled profusely. As Saxby called out for help several people were quickly at the scene. The police were sent for and Saxby was given some medical attention, for the wound to his chest and a head wound. A girl named Miss Scargill said she saw Andrews knock Saxby down. The girl's mother said she saw Andrews holding Saxby on the ground. When the police arrived Andrews fled the scene. A boy named Camberwell said he heard something clasp in the prisoner's hand like a knife. When Andrews was tracked down and arrested, he said:

He attacked me with a knife first or I should not have done it.

Saxby admitted that they both were worse for liquor and when he was on the ground Andrews kicked him several times on the head.

For the defence, Mr Shepherd contended that the wound to Andrews's head was caused as he fell during the struggle and that the wound to his chest was caused by a knife that he himself had in his hand, and that his flesh had been penetrated as he had fallen on the blade. In his own defence Andrews denied having a knife in his hand when the struggle took place. He said that Saxby challenged him to fight three times, which had resulted in him knocking Saxby down. He added that during the struggle that had taken place he had seen a knife in Saxby's hand.

The jury found insufficient evidence to bring in a guilty verdict for using a knife on Saxby, but found Andrews guilty of inflicting grievous bodily harm by kicking. Mr Justice Kennedy committed him to prison for three weeks without hard labour.

LANDLORD RECEIVES SUMMONS FOR SELLING BEER CONTAINING ARSENIC, PENISTONE, APRIL 1901

...due diligence had not been employed in ensuring the speedy withdrawal of the beer from sale at the **Old Crown Inn...**

At the beginning of April 1901, C Brady, Esquire was presiding at Barnsley West Riding Court when John Bradley, landlord of the *Old Crown Inn,* Penistone, was brought up charged under the Food And Drugs Act, with having sold beer containing arsenic, amounting to one quarter of a grain per gallon. The Bench heard that on 26 January the defendant was informed that beer that had been purchased at his inn a few days previously by an official of Penistone Urban District Council, was analysed and found to contain a noticeable quantity of arsenic. When he was told of this anomaly by a council official, Bradley replied:

My Beer is all right.

A second sample was bought at the *Old Crown Inn* on 30 January and found to contain a quarter of a grain of arsenic per gallon. Despite having been warned of the condition of his beer, the defendant continued to sell it. Despite this, somewhat confusingly, the defence was that all reasonable diligence had been used in withdrawing the beer from sale. The defendant said on 23 January he informed the brewery, the owners of the property, of the analysis on the beer supplied by themselves, that had been reported to him. They assured him that the beer they had supplied him with was all right.

When called to give evidence, Mr J Senior, principal partner of the brewing firm, Seth Senior and Sons, of Shepley, the suppliers of the beer, informed the Bench of exactly what the beer contained and the process of brewing it at their brewery. Mr Senior said, they used only malt, hops and invert sugar and barley in browning. He added that they made their own malt. An analytical chemist from Birmingham, Mr W Duncan, said he had traced the arsenic at the brewery to one particular vein of malt, and he attributed it to the use of a certain coal or

A present-day view of the Old Crown *Inn, Penistone.* The author

coke. The Bench considered that due diligence had not been employed in ensuring the speedy withdrawal of the beer from sale at the *Old Crown Inn* and also expressed the opinion that the brewery had similarly not employed adequate steps to withdraw the beer from circulation, as soon as a problem was suspected. However, it was not the brewery up on the charge. The landlord of the *Old Crown Inn*, John Bradley, was given a fine of £20 and costs.

A DANGEROUS GAME OF BILLIARDS, CARLTON, 1902

...*Jolly promptly went over to Parker, who was seated, and struck him a blow on the head with the cue...*

On Wednesday 5 November 1902, Jacob Jolly, a miner, from Carlton, was brought before magistrates at Barnsley West Riding Court. Messrs T Norton, Chairman, H Pigott, W Batty, W Jackson, B Hall and G Blake Walker, were on the Bench. Jolly was summoned by Benjamin Parker, also of Carlton, for an assault, which took place on 20 October. Mr Rideal appeared for the complainant. On the day the alleged assault took place, the two men were playing billiards at *Carlton Main Colliery Club*, when Jolly got vexed because Mr Parker 'potted him in' and Jolly promptly went over to Parker, who was seated, and struck him a blow on the head with the cue, inflicting a wound four inches long, which required stitching. As a result of the injury, Mr Parker had been unable to work for a fortnight and was still incapacitated. The Bench heard that the defendant had promised to pay the complainant £1 a week during his incapacity, but had in fact paid him nothing. Jolly said he hadn't intended to strike Parker on the head and was very sorry for it. Mr Norton said the Bench considered the defendant had administered a violent blow, for which he had no provocation whatever. A fine of £4 and costs was imposed, £3 of which would be given to Benjamin Parker in compensation.

COWARDLY ATTACK AT JUMP, 1903

It is almost remarkable that you did not kill the man.

On Tuesday 3 November 1903, three Jump miners appeared before Barnsley magistrates, having been summoned by another Jump resident for assaulting him on 31 October. Edward Bagnall, Denis Bagnall and William Bottomley, were summoned by miner, John Hallsworth. All three defendants pleaded not guilty. The Bench heard that at 9.10pm on the night of Saturday 31 October, Mr Hallsworth left the public house in Jump where he had been drinking and was on his way home, when Edward Bagnall approached him and immediately caught hold of his body and dragged him to the ground. Then Denis Bagnell joined in the attack and both men set about kicking Mr Hallsworth in the head, causing damage to his eyes, ears, jaw, forehead and scalp. Not content with that, the Bagnalls then kicked Mr Hallsworth in the chest; and considering the injuries he sustained, it appears from witness reports that they then rained kicks all over their victim's body. As Mr Hallsworth lay on the ground William Bottomley joined in the attack and punched him in the mouth. As several people approached the three assailants fled the scene, leaving their victim in what witnesses described as in a state of near death. These witnesses were able to identify Mr Hallsworth's assailants as the three defendants.

In a pathetic attempt at defending his actions, Edward Bagnall said that John Hallsworth challenged him to a fight in the public house and that they then went to a field, 150 yards away, to fight. Bagnall then went on to say that Hallsworth got his coat off and pitched into him before he had a chance. He denied that Mr Hallsworth's injuries were as bad as the Bench had heard. The other two defendants had nothing to say. After a brief discussion, the Chairman, H Piggott, Esquire, said:

> *The Bench are satisfied that the complainant was brutally assaulted and it is a wonder that the three of you are not appearing before us on a graver charge. It is almost remarkable that you did not kill the man. The Bench are determined that in*

cases of violence such as this, when it has been proved up to the hilt, that we exercise what we consider to be our duty by inflicting a severe punishment...

All three defendants were committed to two months with hard labour at the House of Correction at Wakefield.

CARTER'S IMPUDENT THEFT, BARNSLEY, 1904

...he snatched the watch from off the guard she was wearing and refused to return it...

One of the first cases to be heard before magistrates at Barnsley Borough Police Court on the morning of Monday 23 January 1905, concerned the theft of a lady's silver watch the previous September. The Bench heard that George Ware, a carter, of Doncaster Road, admitted his guilt. The complainant, a young girl by the name of Beatrice Higgs, a domestic servant, of 53 Doncaster Road, said that on 18 September 1904, while she was standing talking to Ware, he snatched the watch from off the guard she was wearing and refused to return it and that she had not seen the watch from that day to this.

The chairman, Alderman Raley, asked Miss Higgs if she and the defendant were walking out together, to which Miss Higgs replied that they were not. The Bench were then told that when the defendant was apprehended, he had told the police that when they were out together Miss Higgs had asked him to carry the watch for her as she had no pocket. Ware added:

I afterwards took it to get repaired, but the man I took it to has left the town.

Ware added that he had since found out that the man was now living in Rotherham and that he had written to him but had not received a reply. The Chief Constable said that the watch had not been recovered and if Ware had informed them of what he had done, they would have instigated enquiries. The Bench were clearly not satisfied with Ware's version of events and he was committed to gaol for one month with hard labour.

DRUNKEN POGMOOR LABOURER KICKS AND BITES A POLICEMAN, 1908

...*the Bench was told by the arresting police officers that he had behaved like a madman.*

Pogmoor labourer Edward Bentley was out on the town during Saturday 2 May 1908 and visited several hostelries where he consumed copious amounts of intoxicants. A little after eight o'clock in the evening Bentley was making a nuisance of himself in Shambles Street and it became necessary for the police to be sent for to eject him from a shop there. At 8.20pm, while Police Sergeant Darrington, assisted by Police Constable Herbert, removed him from the shop premises and were in the process of taking him into custody, Bentley tried to strike the sergeant with his fists. On being unsuccessful, he turned his attention to Constable Herbert and immediately bit him on the hand and kicked him on the ankle. The drunken miscreant was successfully subdued and spent the remainder of the weekend in a police cell. Bentley was brought before Barnsley Borough magistrates on Monday morning, charged with being drunk and disorderly and assaulting the police, when the Bench was told by the arresting police officers that he had behaved like a madman. After consulting with Mr C J Tyas and W J Lowrance, the chairman, W E Raley, Esquire, handed down a fine of 5*s*. for the drunkenness and 10*s*. and costs for the assault.

CHAPTER 3

Early George V Through the Roaring Twenties

ILLEGAL TAKING OF BETS, HOYLAND COMMON, JUNE 1912

...that, as well as seeing Burgin being handed betting slips, he had also seen people giving him money.

In the early afternoon of Monday 10 June 1912, Wilson Burgin, of Hoyland Common was about his business collecting betting slips from numerous clients throughout the district. Unbeknown to Mr Burgin his comings and goings were being closely watched by Police Constable Geary, who made a note in his pocket book that between 12.30pm and 2.00pm, he saw Burgin receive betting slips, which he put in his jacket pocket, from eighteen women and twenty-eight men. The next day, Constable Geary made notes to the effect that between one o'clock and 1.40pm he saw six men and sixteen women hand Burgin betting slips. In his notes concerning the events on both days, Constable Geary wrote that as well as seeing Burgin being handed betting slips he had also seen people giving him money. Burgin was followed home by Constable Geary and told that he would be reported for taking bets. Burgin replied:

Well, what am I to do? I got stopped on the railway eighteen months ago, and I am a cripple for life.

When Wilson Burgin was brought before Barnsley magistrates, he was described as a bookmaker. In the evidence presented against Burgin, Sergeant Robinson said:

For the past eighteen months the defendant has done nothing but take bets. He stands at the point where four roads meet and is within thirty yards of his home, and can command a view of the approach from four different positions. Every now and then, when he gets a few slips – he goes down to his house with them. He is always careful not to go far from his home.

Burgin was indicted on two charges of taking bets for illegal gambling, one for each day and pleaded guilty. He was fined £10 and costs.

SENT TO GAOL FOR DRAWING ANOTHER'S WAGES, PLATTS COMMON, JUNE 1912

On being given the money to which he was not entitled, Rhodes immediately absconded and was eventually run to ground at Pontefract...

Machineman Edward Rhodes, from Platts Common, pleaded guilty to a charge of stealing £3 7s. 5d., when he was brought before Barnsley magistrates, on Friday 6 September 1912. The stolen money was the property of the Hoyland Silkstone Colliery Co. Ltd.

Hoyland Silkstone Colliery. Walkers Newsagents collection

On Tuesday 11 June, Rhodes went to work on the afternoon shift at the Hoyland Silkstone Colliery, calling in at the office as was his usual practice before starting his shift and was signed on by William Baldwin, the timekeeper. He earned 6*s* 11*d.* that day. He didn't work on any other day that week, so all he was entitled to receive was one shift's money. On the following Saturday, Rhodes went to the office just as Mr Baldwin was engaged in getting the pay checks ready and he was told that his paying out check was No.*493*, for which he was asked to call later. When he returned sometime later, Mr Baldwin was otherwise engaged. Rhodes asked for Check No.*492*, which was duly handed to him by the deputy Edward Palmer and when he presented the check at the pay office he received £3 14*s. 4d.*, £3 7*s. 5d.* more than he was entitled to receive for his own check, No.*493*. About an hour later when the man who was entitled to receive the money for check No.*492* presented himself at the pay office, it was found that his check had already been given out and the money drawn. On being given the money to which he was not entitled Rhodes immediately absconded and was eventually run to ground at Pontefract, where he was arrested, on Saturday 31 May. He told Police Constable Bell that he was very sorry that he took the money and added that he did not know what he was doing at the time. Rhodes told the Bench that this was the first time he had been in trouble in his life and asked if they would deal with him leniently. He was sent to gaol for one month.

A BARNSLEY BEAST – HIS 109th APPEARANCE IN COURT, JUNE 1919

…He is a beast and should be sent away for as long a period as your Worships can possibly send him.

Sydney Newton was a well-known character in the Barnsley district, one of those individuals that seem to have been a feature of most towns in England, both in days gone by and right up to the present day: a petty criminal, habitually in trouble and occasionally referred to by some as 'a loveable rogue'. However, it would seem that, far from being a lovable rogue, the vast majority of upstanding Barnsley citizens of the day seemed more inclined to view Sydney Newton as nothing but a nuisance, and those who had been at the receiving end of his lewd and lascivious conduct could no doubt find a few choice words to describe their tormentor, and lovable rogue did not enter their vocabulary when it came to their views of an apt description of Newton.

On Sunday afternoon, 1 March 1919, Newton was arrested by Police Constable Spires, at Old Mill, following a complaint he had received from a young woman. On Monday morning Newton came up before magistrates at Barnsley West Riding Court, charged with indecent conduct. The Bench was chaired by W Dutson, Esquire. Up to his appearance in Court that morning, Newton, who had first been convicted in 1881, had served ninety terms of imprisonment, totalling fourteen years. Major Carrington (the magistrates' clerk) said:

> ...for various offences the prisoner has served three sentences of twelve months each, three of six months, nineteen of three months, three of two months and forty-three of one month. This is his 109th appearance before magistrates...

Superintendent McDonald said there had been many complaints of this class of offence in various parts of the Division. There had been one at Wombwell recently and police were satisfied that Newton was the man concerned. At the conclusiuon of his evidence, the superintendent added:

> He is a beast and should be sent away for as long a period as your Worships can possibly send him.

Newton, after expressing regret for committing the offence on the young woman, asked the Bench not to send him to the Sessions, adding that he would rather be sent to a home. In addressing the prisoner, Mr Dutson said:

> The Bench is very sorry we cannot deal with you more severely. You will go to prison for three months.

STAIRFOOT CONFECTIONER IN A JAM, DECEMBER 1919

...Mr Potts had been ill resulting in him being unable to give proper consideration to his business.

On Wednesday 7 January 1920, Arthur Potts, confectioner, of Stairfoot, stood in the dock before Barnsley magistrates at the West Riding Court, where he pleaded guilty to breaches of the Jam Prices Order, of September 1919.

The court heard from Police Superintendent McDonald that the scheduled price for a 2*lb.* jar of strawberry jam was 2*s.* 2½ *d.* On 23 December 1919, at the request of the police, a woman named Mrs Senior, of 15 Victoria Street, went to Mr Potts's shop and purchased a 2*lb.* jar of strawberry jam, for which she was charged 2*s.* 8*d.* A copy of the controlled prices was not exhibited in the shop.

Acting for the defence, Mr G R Brumfitt, said that Mr Potts was a confectioner and did not sell much jam. However, when it came to his knowledge that jam was controlled, Mr Potts had I, immediately obtained a price list from the local food office. This notice was in the shop at the time Mrs Senior had made her purchase of the jam but it had not been posted up. Mr Brumfitt added that Mr Potts had been ill resulting in him being unable to give proper consideration to his business.

The Bench deliberated for a few moments, before the chairman, T Norton, Esquire, who pointed out that the defendant was liable to a fine of £100. Mr Norton then added that on this occasion the Bench would only impose a fine of 20*s.* and trusted the defendant would be more careful in future.

FOR LARCENY AND FALSE PRETENCES CHARGES MR JUSTICE AVORY GIVES WIGGING TO AN HABITUAL CRIMINAL, 1920

...he had been released before completing his sentence, having made a promise that he would abstain from crime.

On Wednesday 5 May 1920, thirty-nine-year-old, labourer Arthur Beaumont, appeared at Leeds Assizes, before Mr

Justice Avory, on charges of false pretences and larceny, at Barnsley. He pleaded guilty.

Beaumont's record showed that he had been committing crimes of a similar nature to those described above, for several years. He had fourteen previous convictions and in 1914 he was sentenced to three years' penal servitude and five years' preventative detention for being an habitual criminal. However, he had been released before completing his sentence, having made a promise that he would abstain from crime. In a statement which the prisoner handed to his Lordship, he alleged that the reason he was standing in the dock was that the authorities at Durham, where he had served his sentence had prevented him from obtaining employment by disclosing details of his past criminal activities. His Lordship said he did not believe this to be the case and that the prisoner was trying to impose on him, just as he had imposed on the public and on the prison authorities. His Lordship told Beaumont:

> *I am taking into account some nine or ten other charges to which you have pleaded guilty, in addition to those of obtaining by false pretences from Grace Scott of Barnsley, on April 10th, food to the value of 6s. with intent to defraud, a similar offence in respect to Alice Ibbeson, on February 2nd, and the larceny of a gold albert from Tom Dagger, at Barnsley, on 3rd February...*

In addition to these charges, Mr Justice Avory said that the prisoner had left no doubt in his mind that he was indeed an habitual criminal. His Lordship then replicated the sentence Beaumont had received in 1914, by sentencing him to three years' penal servitude and five years' preventative detention.

ATTEMPTED MURDER, CUDWORTH, 1923

...*Florence Siddall struck her brother-in-law on the head with a poker, which quietened him down.*

On the afternoon of Thursday 16 August 1923, the streets around Cudworth were buzzing with the news that a murderous attack had occurred involving a young miner on his wife. On Friday 17 August, twenty-nine-year-old Albert Henry Beardshaw, of Rockingham Street, Fitzwilliam, near Hemsworth, was brought up in custody in the dock at Barnsley West Riding Court, with his head swathed in bandages. He was charged with the attempted murder of his wife, Sarah Ann.

Outlining the background to the case, Police Superintendent Blacker explained that Beardshaw and his wife were living apart. A maintenance order had been granted against the prisoner but he had not contributed any money towards his wife's upkeep. Mrs Beardshaw was living with her mother and married sister (Mrs Florence Siddall) at 96 The Avenue, Newtown, Cudworth.

On the morning the attack on Mrs Bearshaw took place she received a letter from her husband, asking her to meet him at Grimethorpe, and threatening if she did not do so she and the children would not live long. The letter read:

Dear Sarah,

Just a few lines to you and the children, hoping you are all in good health, as it leaves me nearly off my head. Well, I want you to meet me at the top of Grimethorpe fields at 3 p.m. tomorrow (Wednesday) and remember, if you do not come, well you and the children will not live long, and also those who have parted us will go under, as I am desperate, so don't forget. I have a good job to go to on Thursday away from here altogether, and I will work my fingers to the bone if only you will give me the chance to prove it. Remember, when you have read this letter, understand, throw It into the fire at once. Don't let anybody see it, as it is yours and my last chance, so do as I ask you. From your broken-hearted husband, Albert. Good-night. Remember, don't let me in.

Mrs Bradshaw did not comply with her husband's request and at about 1.50pm on the day after the requested meeting the prisoner called at 96 The Avenue and Mrs Siddall answered the knock on the door. Albert Beardshaw was standing on the doorstep and he said he wanted to see his wife as he had some money for her. Mrs Siddall left Beardshaw standing at the door, and went to fetch her sister. When Mrs Beardshaw went to the door her husband immediately attacked her with a razor, inflicting very serious wounds. She let out a scream and her mother and sister ran to her aid. When they arrived at the door they saw Sarah Beardshaw, covered with blood and struggling with her husband. She made a desperate attempt to get away and while her sister and mother grappled with the struggling man, Florence Siddall struck her brother-in-law on the head with a poker, which quietened him down. The razor was taken from him and the police were called and arrived within minutes. When Beardshaw was arrested he made no reply. Dr L Sugare, who was acting as locum for Dr Walsh, was sent for, and he found Mrs Beardshaw badly cut.

Sarah Beardshaw's wounds consisted of, two cuts on the back of the neck – 4*ins.* long, and the other 2*ins* long and superficial. There was another cut on the lobe of the right ear and one on the right temple, 1*ins* long. There was a deep cut, from the tip of the chin to the angle of the left jaw and a superficial wound 5*ins* long on the left side of the neck and several other minor injuries on the left side of the shoulder. There was also a cut on the ball of the thumb 3/4*ins* in length. At the conclusion of this evidence Beardshaw was remanded until Friday, when further witnesses were called. Beardshaw claimed that he was inebriated when the alleged attack took place but several witnesses, including Fred Siddall, the defendant's brother-in-law, who had come downstairs from his sick bed when he heard the commotion taking place downstairs, and Police Constable Garbutt, who took Beardshaw in charge, maintained he was perfectly sober. Beardshaw said:

> *I had been drinking at the* Star Hotel *at Cudworth and there were some men in there who know it. I could pick them out, but I don't know their names.*

At the end of the proceedings, Beardshaw was committed to take his trial at the Assizes.

Albert Henry Beardshaw's case came up at Leeds Assizes, on Thursday 6 December, where the evidence given at Barnsley West Riding Court was repeated and additional witnesses were called. The medical officer at Armley Gaol, Dr Worsley, said, having observed the prisoner, he had formed the opinion that although he was mentally unstable, he was not insane. The jury found Beardshaw guilty of attempted murder. He was sentenced to seven years' penal servitude.

OFFENDING CHARABANC DRIVER, CARLTON LANE, 1925

...he had a narrow escape of being knocked down.

On Friday 20 February 1925, motor-driver, Alfred Howe, was summoned to appear at Barnsley's West Riding Court, charged with failing to give audible warning of his approach, whilst driving a charabanc. Police Constable Wright said that on the night of 31 January, he was on patrol near Carlton Lane schools, when the defendant's char-a-banc came round a blind bend and the driver did not sound his horn. Constable Wright, who was in the road, said he had a narrow escape of being knocked down. The defendant, who was represented by Mr A Smith, strongly denied the charge against him but the Bench was satisfied that the case had been proven and imposed a fine of 20*s*. and costs.

CHAPTER 4

Nineteen Thirties, Forties and Fifties

HIGHAM LODGER GUILTY OF THEFT, 1932

...Land had cleared out his belongings and absconded with a 10s. note...

On Monday 9 January 1933, W Humphries, Esquire, was chairing the Bench at Barnsley West Riding Police Court when labourer John W Land, of no fixed abode was brought up to answer to a charge of stealing a 10*s.* note from J W Fearn, with whom he used to lodge.

Police Superintendent Varley said that Land used to lodge with Mr Fearn at Higham. Mr Fearn had been collecting for a Christmas club and the money, totalling 36*s.*, had been put in a cupboard. On 3 December, Land was alone in the house, and when Mr Fearn returned home had cleared out his belongings and absconded with a 10*s.* note which was missing from the cupboard. The Bench also learned that Land was wanted by the Wakefield City Police on a warrant over a wife maintenance order and would be handed over to them once the case had been heard. Land, who was originally from Wakefield, had been living in Barnsley for the previous nine years. PC Gwinnett said that on being charged with stealing the 10*s.*, Land had replied:

I'm sorry. I took it on the spur of the moment.

The police had no previous record against Land and he had been unemployed for the last fourteen months, having previously worked at the smokeless fuel depot at Barugh. The Chairman, Mr Humphries, told him:

As this is your first offence the Bench do not desire to send you to prison. You will be bound over in the sum of £5 for twelve months and will have the costs of this court appearance to pay.

Following the hearing, Land was immediately handed over to Wakefield City Police.

MEAT PURVEYOR RECEIVES HEAVY FINE FOR SELLING MEAT UNFIT 'FOR THE GOOD OF MAN' AT HOYLAND MARKET, 1933

Dr Allott said that the meat he had examined was putrefied and utterly unfit for human consumption.

On Friday 17 March 1933, a meat purveyor, named Eric Holt, of Grimesthorpe, Sheffield, was severely dealt with by the Bench at Barnsley West Riding Police Court, when he pleaded not guilty to having exposed for sale, at Hoyland Market, meat that was unsound and unfit 'for the good of man'.

Prosecuting on behalf of Hoyland Nether Urban District Council, Mr S Raley, said:

... at 7.30pm on Saturday February 11 the Sanitary Inspector for the Hoyland Nether Urban District Council was making a tour of the Market Place, apposite the Strafford Arms. *On a stall under the supervision of a man named Ben Jaques, of High Green, who was in the employ of Holt, he noticed three pieces of meat that appeared to him to be of a greenish colour, flabby in appearance and putrified.*

When the Sanitary Inspector, John Yates, asked Jaques if he could sell him some of the meat, having agreed to do so, the inspector revealed his identity and ordered the meat to be put on one side. This same meat, consisting of four large pieces of carcass, was subsequently condemned to destruction by Nathaniel Mell, JP, it having been examined by Dr H R L Allott, the Medical Officer of Health, who also expressed the opinion that the meat was not fit for human consumption. In addressing the Bench, Mr Raley said that he hoped they would inflict the maximum penalty if they found the case proved, as Hoyland was a distressed area and consequently the people bought their provisions in the lowest market.

Sanitary Inspector John Yates said that in Hoyland they had been experiencing great trouble from butchers who came from outside the area and sold their meat in Hoyland Market, undercutting local traders, who killed almost the whole of their meat in the district. Dr Allott said that the meat he had examined was putrefied and utterly unfit for human consumption.

The stall attendant, Ben Jaques, said he had had thirty years in the trade and with regard to one leg of mutton, he would have willingly taken it home and eaten it for his own dinner. He had not noticed the condition of the other three pieces. Holt said the pieces of meat in question had all been taken out of the refrigerator by mistake. He obtained all his meat from the Sheffield abattoir, which was all guaranteed and he had no intention to offer meat that was not sound for sale.

The condition of the meat being offers for sale in Hoyland Market seemed to contradict Holt's assertions. The chairman, Alderman Herbert Smith, told Holt:

The Bench is determined that you shall not take advantage of the poverty of people in distressed areas. You are liable to a fine of £60, and we cannot do less than order you to pay a fine of £20 and the costs.

MEN BROUGHT UP BEFORE BARNSLEY MAGISTRATES DURING FESTIVE SEASON, 1937

...had apparently been over indulgent during the festive season...

On New Year's Eve 1937, W Humphries, Esquire (chairman), Nathaniel Mell, Esquire, G Brigs, Esquire and Captain Allott, were sitting at Barnsley West Riding Police Court, when several men who had apparently been over indulgent during the festive season were brought up before them. Walter Parrish, miner, of Royston and twenty-year-old miner Ronald

Pearson of West Melton, were each fined 5s. for having been drunk and disorderly. For using obscene language, labourer Herbert Semley of Worsbrough Bridge, was also fined the sum of 5s., while for having used violent and abusive language, miner, George Merrils of Cudworth and pit hand, John G Allott, were fined 10s. and 7s. 6d. respectively.

GREAT HOUGHTON BOOKMAKER'S RUNNER RECEIVES HEAVY FINE, 1938

...Arthur was spotted taking betting slips in Cross Street, Great Houghton ...

On Wednesday 27 July 1938, Walter Arthur, described as a bookmaker's runner, stood in the dock at Barnsley West Riding Police Court, charged with street betting. The Bench were told by Police Constable Cooper that Arthur was spotted taking betting slips in Cross Street, Great Houghton and when arrested said:

Let's get it over and done with.

When searched, Arthur had in his possession thirteen betting slips relating to thirty-one bets and 20s. in cash. The chairman, G H Norton, Esquire, told Arthur:

You were here in 1934, and in 1936 you were fined £10 then, and now it will be £15.

LUNDWOOD HOUSEWIFE LEARNS THAT THE LAW SAYS FINDING'S NOT KEEPING, 1945

...that if it had not been for the beer she had drank, she would have returned the 10s. note to its owner.

On Saturday 29 December 1945, twenty-five-year-old Mrs Olive Ullah, of Priory Road, Lundwood, was seen to pick up a 10s. banknote which had been inadvertently dropped by Mrs Betty Nightingale, of 65 Rotherham Road, West Melton, in

Barnsley market place. As a result of finding the banknote and having made no attempt to restore it to its owner, Mrs Ullah found herself in court on a charge of 'stealing by finding'.

On Monday 31 December, Chief Inspector Blunt told the Bench at Barnsley Borough Magistrates' Court, chaired by Alderman Edward Sheerien. Chief Inspector Blunt said:

> *Mrs Nightingale and her sister were in a pie stall in the market place, when she dropped a 10s. note. Ullah, who was standing there, picked it up and went away. She was seen later by Nightingale who said to her, 'You know that 10s. note you found. It is mine.' Ullah replied, 'I haven't got it now.'*

When the police arrived Ullah said:

> *It is my 10s. I dropped it.*

Ullah eventually handed 7s. 3½d. over to the police, saying that was all that remained of the 10s.

Detective Constable Sagar said Ullah had told him that she had visited several pubs with a friend and had a lot to drink and that if it had not been for the beer she had drank, she would have returned the 10s. note to its owner. The Bench fined Olive Ullah 20s. for stealing by finding and they also directed that the money found on Ullah should be returned to Mrs Nightingale.

STAIRFOOT MAN FINED FOR USING INDECENT LANGUAGE, 1946

I didn't notice what I was saying.

On Friday 12 April 1946, Nathanial Mell, Esquire, was chairing the Bench at Barnsley West Riding Magistrates' Court, with one other magistrate, A Francis, Esquire, seated alongside him, when twenty-one-year-old Stanley Spenceley, of 17 Stanley Street, Stairfoot, appeared before them, charged with having used indecent language in a public place. The Bench were told by Police Constable Hodges that on 17

March, he heard the defendant swear no fewer than eleven times and when stopped by himself, Spenceley replied:

I didn't notice what I was saying.

After a few moments consultation with Mr Francis, Mr Mell informed Spencely that he would be fined 20*s.* plus costs.

DRUNKEN MAN GOES ON WINDOW BREAKING SPREE, BARNSLEY, 1947

... saw Towey strike and break the window of the shop in Sheffield Road by striking it with his walking stick.

Police Superintendent Legg, described the prisoner in the dock appearing before Barnsley magistrates, on Monday 19 May 1947, as being, 'alright when sober'. The Bench heard that forty-one-year-old labourer Edward Towey, of Thornton Road, Kendray, when drunk, seemed to have developed a penchant for smashing windows. Towey was charged with being drunk and disorderly on 15 April and doing wilful damage to plate glass windows at 71 Sheffield Road (valued at £12), at a milk bar in Peel Street (valued at £10), at the *Industry Inn*, Baker Street (valued at £5), and at 132 Doncaster Road (valued at 15*s.*), all on the same night.

Police Superintendent Legg said the windows were broken between 11.30pm and 4.15am, when Towey was found crouching under the cemetery wall in Pindar Oaks Street. One witness saw Towey strike and break the window of the shop in Sheffield Road by striking it with his walking stick. When charged, Towey was in such a bad state that through the semi-coherent babble that he uttered it soon became clear that he did not know whether he had broken the windows or not. Towey pleaded guilty and was sentenced to one month's imprisonment on the first charge, three months' on each of the next three charges and one month on each on the last charge, sentences to run concurrently.

A SWEET AND FRUITY TALE OF A BROKEN NOSE AND TWO LOVELY BLACK EYES, JUMP 1948

...her face was disfigured and swollen and her nose misshaped.

In April 1948, Mrs Gladys Victoria Gregory, of 19 Milton Square, Jump found herself at a variance of opinion with her husband Alfred over the division of a pound of dolly mixtures and six oranges between the children of her first marriage and those of her present one. The ensuing fight between husband and wife resulted in Mrs Gregory receiving two black eyes and a broken nose.

On Friday 9 April, forty-three-year-old bricklayer Alfred E Gregory was brought before the Bench at Barnsley West Riding Magistrates' Court, charged with occasioning bodily harm to his wife. Police Constable Moran said that when Mrs Gregory was seen at the Police Station, her face was disfigured and swollen and her nose misshaped. The Bench heard that when Mrs Gregory told her husband she thought the sweets and oranges had been divided unfairly between the children, he flung the sweets at her and struck her with his fist.

Gregory was defended by Mr D P McKenzie. According to the defendant, after dividing the sweets and oranges, his wife had grabbed him by the throat and scratched him about the neck. In his struggle to defend himself his elbow caught her on the nose. He then gave her a 'back-hander'. Mrs Gregory admitted to the Bench that she later found that her husband had shared the sweets and oranges fairly.

Gregory was ordered to pay a fine of 20*s.* and costs.

GAOLED FOR STEALING FROM CARS, BARNSLEY 1949

...when arrested he had commented that he was surprised how easy it was to steal from cars.

Following a spate of thefts from parked vehicles in Barnsley town centre, a special watch was being kept. On Friday 23

December 1949, Detective Constables Pask and Green saw a man trying car doors in the car park in Wellington Street. When her was arrested the man made a voluntary statement to police, which resulted in his appearance before Barnsley magistrates on Thursday 5 January 1950. Thirty-three-year-old coal-cutter John Preece, of Brittania Street, Barnsley pleaded guilty to two charges of stealing articles worth £25 from cars parked in Wellington Street during the previous December. He also asked for fourteen other similar offences to be taken into account, which he had committed over the previous twelve months.

Police Superintendent Legg said that on Friday 23 December Hugh Shaw, of Willy Road, Carlton, parked his car in Wellington Street and when he returned to it he found a clock and 400 cigarettes were missing. Preece was arrested later that same day when he was observed by detectives to be acting suspiciously in the car park. The Bench were told that this was Preece's first offence and when arrested he had commented that he was surprised how easy it was to steal from cars. Preece was employed at Woolley Colliery, where he earned £7 a week. In giving the Bench's decision, the chairman (the Mayor, Councillor W Hunt) told Preece he was lucky not to be sent to prison. He was given a fine of £50, with the stipulation that the fine should be paid in instalments of £1 a week, in default of which he would be imprisoned for six months.

DODWORTH SOLDIER GAOLED FOR STEALING VEHICLES AND SUNDRY ITEMS, 1950

...Lomax made a voluntary statement in which he admitted taking the vehicle, the property of British Road Services.

On Thursday 20 April 1950, a twenty-year-old soldier, from Intake Crescent, Dodworth, was sent to prison for twelve months by magistrates at Barnsley Borough Court, for stealing a long distance transport lorry from Barnsley Town Hall car park. The lorry was laden with 320*lbs* of butter. It was stolen

Barnsley Town Hall, where Harry Lomax stole a butter-laden lorry from the car park. Author's collection

on the night of Tuesday 7 March. Harry Lomax was charged with taking away the motor vehicle without the owner's consent; with stealing bed linen and sundry articles; with stealing 96*lbs* of butter and with stealing a postal draft worth £ 8*s*. 6*d*.

Police Superintendent Legg said Lomax made a voluntary statement in which he admitted taking the vehicle, the property of British Road Services. The Bench heard that Lomax drove the lorry to Thurgoland and unloaded some of its cargo, then drove it to Worsbrough Bridge, where he abandoned it. Lomax also admitted to having stolen a car, on 26 March, the property of Mr John Edward Bailey, of Warner Avenue, Pogmoor, from outside a house at Pogmoor, which he drove to Mapplewell. The car contained a suitcase in which was packed bed linen and other goods valued at £12 13*s*. 11*d*. Lomax took the goods contained in the suitcase to Carr Green Lane, Mapplewell and gave them to his brother and sister-in-law, who lived there. The postal draft was stolen on 17 February from Mr R Bailey of Blythe Street, Wombwell. These admissions were made by Lomax when he was interviewed by police at his army camp. In addition to being sent to prison,

Lomax was fined £1 on each of two charges for driving a motor vehicle without a driving licence or insurance and he was disqualified from driving for two years.

POTATO THIEVES GIVEN A HEAVY FINE, DARFIELD, SEPTEMBER, 1952

Farmers depend on potatoes as part of their living and upon honest people being about when they leave their potatoes unattended.

On Tuesday September 30 1952, farmer James Cravan of Edderthorpe Farm, Darfield, left newly harvested potatoes at the edge of a field on his farm. At 4.45.am the following day he noticed a British Road Services lorry parked in the lane next to the field and subsequently discovered some potatoes had been stolen. Mr Cravan reported the theft to the police. Police observations were kept and on 4 October at 4.30am two lorries were seen parked in the lane and their registration numbers noted. When the numbers were checked at the British Road Services depot at Cudworth it was discovered that the two drivers had runs that would take them past Mr Cravan's potato field. The drivers, thirty-five-year-old Ian McPherson, of Cranbrook Street, Barnsley and twenty-seven-year-old James F Moore, of Churchfield Crescent, Cudworth were interviewed by police. When McPherson was approached he produced a sack and a half of potatoes belonging to Mr Cravan and made a statement admitting the theft. McPherson's statement also implicated Moore. However, when Moore was approached, he denied being involved. Moore was shown a copy of McPherson's statement and when charged with theft of the potatoes he said:

I was in bed that night.

In December 1952, McPherson and Moore were brought up before magistrates at Barnsley West Riding Court. Mr F Taylor prosecuting was moved to comment:

This was a particularly mean theft. Farmers depend on potatoes as part of their living and upon honest people being about when they leave their potatoes unattended.

Mr A S McKenzie, defending McPherson, said in mitigation:

My client is very ashamed of himself. However, he would like me to point out that on the second occasion when the lorries were seen, he and Mr Moore had only pulled in because of a faulty rear light. There was no intention to steal on that occasion.

Moore asked that one case of stealing three sacks of potatoes valued at 9*s.* be taken into consideration. He added:

I am also ashamed of myself. I have by my actions ruined my chances of getting into the West Riding Police Force.

McPherson and Moore were each fined £5.

CHAPTER 5

Animals, Fowls, Birds and Game Matters

TRESPASS IN PURSUIT OF GAME, NEAR CARLTON, 1857

...laid down in the corner of the wood with his hand on a single-barreled gun.

George Wilkinson, of Mapplewell, appeared at Barnsley courthouse, on Wednesday 24 February 1857, charged with trespassing on land belonging to Lord Wharncliffe. On the Bench were Thomas Taylor, Esquire, Godfrey Wentworth, Esquire and J S Stanhope, Esquire. Evidence against Wilkinson was given by game-watcher Emmanuel Cherry. Cherry said he was watching in Norroyd's Wood, near Carlton on the night of Friday 19 February, when he came across the defendant, laid down in the corner of the wood with his hand on a single-barreled gun. Wilkinson was taken in charge without resistance. After a few moments discussion the chairman said the Bench was satisfied Wilkinson was in the wood for an unlawful purpose. He was fined £2 or in default to be committed for two months to Wakefield House of Correction.

GOOSE STOLEN AT CAWTHORNE, 1865

Shaw admitted that he had picked it up in a turnip field.

On Monday 14 August 1865, Aaron Shaw appeared in the dock at Barnsley courthouse before Rev H B Cooke, charged with stealing a goose. John Wilkinson of Cawthorne, the owner of the goose, reported it stolen to police sergeant Hay on Saturday 12 August. Sergeant Hay told the court that having received information about the robbery he had made enquiries in the district and discovered that Aaron Shaw had been offering a goose for sale. He apprehended Shaw in Cawthorne Lane and when charged with having stolen the goose, Shaw admitted that he had picked it up in a turnip field. Having been found guilty of the offence, Shaw was committed to Wakefield House of Correction for one month.

POACHING AFFRAY AT CUDWORTH, 1868

If you don't go away I'll blow your brains out.

William Atha, brickmaker, was brought up before Mr Justice Lush, at the Yorkshire Summer Assizes, held at Leeds Town Hall, on Monday 10 August 1868. He was indicted on two counts: for feloniously wounding James Jagger, on 5 July, at Cudworth, with intent to do him some grievous bodily harm; and also with assaulting him, with intent to resist his lawful apprehension. Mr Blackburn prosecuted. The prisoner was not defended.

The court heard that James Jagger, gamekeeper, was employed by Messrs Newman and Wright, who had shooting rights over some land in the vicinity of Cudworth. On the night of 4/5 July, Jagger was in the company of another keeper, Emmanuel Cherry, keeping watch. At about twelve-thirty, they heard a gunshot and as they went in the direction from where it came they heard another shot. When they arrived at a field called the Old Pasture they saw a man but this was not the prisoner. Jagger and Cherry seized the man and took him into the road, as they did so William Atha came out of a hedge with a gun in his hand and told them to stop. They stood for a while, then Jagger said to Atha:

Don't be a fool; don't shoot.

To which Atha replied:

If you don't go away I'll blow your brains out.

The keepers then let go of the man and he went back into the Old Pasture with Atha. Almost immediately a shot rang out and Jagger and Cherry ran into the field and seized hold of Atha. Jagger threw him upon the ground, holding him there for almost ten minutes. Then the other man came back on the scene and attacked Cherry, beating him to the ground. Jagger got hold of the man and threw him to the ground on top of Atha. Atha got up and struck Jagger a blow on the head with the butt of his gun. The force of the blow was such that it rendered Jagger insensible. Atha again struck Jagger on the head and kicked him, fracturing one of his ribs. Cherry who was lying nearby, had also been seriously injured by Atha's companion, his injuries included a broken arm. Atha and his companion disappeared into the night. Jagger and Cherry made their way to their homes with some difficulty. Jagger's injuries were such that for several days following the attack his life was in danger.

On the night following the attack, Atha had a hare in his possession. During a conversation with a friend of his, overheard by others, Atha said he had a fight with the keepers and had left them for dead, and that he had broken his gun with striking at them. Atha's description was given to police and he was quickly apprehended. When charged, Atha denied any knowledge of the incident, maintaining he was asleep in bed at the time. That was the case against him.

In summing up, Mr Justice Lush said:

> *In point of law the prisoner had a right to resist apprehension, because it had not been shown that the keepers had any right to take him into custody. Thus, the only question for the jury would be whether the prisoner used greater violence than was necessary to deliver himself from the custody of the keepers.*

The jury found Atha guilty of unlawful wounding. In passing sentence his Lordship said the jury had taken a view of the case which was in the prisoner's favour; for if they had found him guilty of the major offence, he should have sent him to penal servitude. Instead, Atha was sentenced to fifteen months' imprisonment.

CRUELTY TO A PIT PONY, MONK BRETTON COLLIERY, 1902

... *this was the worst case of cruelty ever to have been brought before them.*

William Shepherd, a labourer at Monk Bretton Colliery, was brought before Barnsley magistrates, charged with cruelty to a pit pony on 7 November. Mr Rideal prosecuted and Mr J Raley defended. Shepherd pleaded not guilty. Mr Rideal said:

> *This is as shocking a case of cruelty as has ever been before this court ... As the pony did not succeed in wrenching some rails from the ground, Shepherd, who had nothing at all to do with the pony, went to a place where a man named Atkinson was working and, picking up a pick shaft, said he was going to thrash the pony with it. Atkinson told Shepherd that he would get into trouble and took the pick shaft away from him. Shepherd then went and procured a piece of wood, and broke it over the pony, causing it to fall down. He then picked up a piece of the wood and poked the*

animal in a most shameful manner. Fortunately the pony is alive and it is hoped it will still live…

George Holmes, who was in charge of the pony, confirmed the evidence presented by Mr Rideal and added that he had begged Shepherd not to beat the pony. Mr Smith, a veterinary surgeon, during his evidence, emphasised the seriousness of the injuries and said they had most likely been caused by a stick. He added that after he examined the pony it was clear that if the point of the wood had penetrated another quarter of an inch, the bowels of the animal would have been injured. Evidence for the prosecution was also given by Reuben Atkinson and John Birch. Mr J L Marshall, manager of Monk Bretton Colliery, said he had never seen a worse case of cruel treatment. In Shepherd's defence, Mr Rideal said that his client admitted having beaten the pony to make it work, but not cruelly. He never prodded it. The Bench were of the opinion that this was the worst case of cruelty ever to have been brought before them. The chairman added they were of the opinion it would be absurd to inflict a fine and committed Shepherd to one month at Wakefield prison, with hard labour.

GAME TRESPASS ON EARL FITZWILLIAM'S LAND, BILLINGLEY, 1908

They put up a rabbit, which was caught and Spendlove was seen to pocket it.

Three young pony drivers from Broomhill, William Edward Steel, James Clarke and Tom Spendlove, found themselves in the dock at Barnsley West Riding Court, on Wednesday 5 May 1908, charged with trespass in search of game, on Earl Fitzwilliam's land at Billingley, on Friday 28 April. Mr Rideal, prosecuting on behalf of Lord Fitzwilliam, told the Bench that at about seven o'clock on Good Friday evening, the three youths were spotted by one of the Earl's gamekeepers, John Taylor, ranging a field with two 'snap dogs'. Spendlove had a catapult. They put up a rabbit, which was caught and Spendlove was seen to pocket it. The three lads made off on

William Charles de Meuron, 7th Earl Fitzwilliam, KCVO, CBE, DSO, JP, DL (1872–1943), seen here in his major's uniform, with one of the guns of the Wentworth battery of the Royal Artillery. Roy Young collection

seeing the keeper but two of them, Clarke and Steel, were caught. All three pleaded guilty. In mitigation, Spendlove said they were out walking and the dogs happened to find a rabbit. They were each given a fine of 10s. and costs.

GAME TRESPASS AT CAWTHORNE, 1916

The keepers admitted that they did not get nearer the man than twenty yards.

On Wednesday 19 January 1916, magistrates at Barnsley West Riding Court heard a case brought by Mr J M Spencer Stanhope of Cannon Hall, against Alfred Hartley, for game trespass in Low Land plantation, Cawthorne.

Mr Rideal prosecuted. Evidence was provided by Mr Spencer Stanhope's under-keeper, Alexander Hughes and James Armstrong, a keeper in the employ of Lord Allendale.

The court heard that at about 5.00pm, on the afternoon of Monday 10 January, they saw Hartley in the middle of the plantation, accompanied by a liver and white dog and carrying a gun. When they were within twenty and thirty yards of the defendant they heard a gun being fired. It was alleged that the defendant saw the keepers coming towards him and ran away. The keepers found a dead pheasant lying nearby. It was still warm. They said they had no doubt that the man they had seen fleeing was the defendant.

Mr J Raley defended Hartley. He said that the keepers had made a mistake with regard to the identity of the man they had seen in the wood, on the evening in question, and that his client was at home in Barugh at the time of the alleged incident. The keepers admitted that they did not get nearer the man than twenty yards. That day the sun had set at 4.08pm, almost an hour before the defendant was allegedly spotted by the keepers, and as the shades of night was falling there was no moon. Hartley denied that he was in Low Land plantation on the day in question. A witness was called. Taxidermist Joseph Walker said that in addition to his principal occupation, he also repaired guns and that from Saturday 8 January to the following Friday, he had Alfred Hartley's gun at his house for repair. Despite the lack of supportable evidence against the defendant, chairman J T Field, Esquire said the Bench had no doubt about the case and ordered Hartley to pay a fine of 40*s*. and the witnesses expenses.

DRUNKEN MAN SHOOTS AT DOG WITH A REVOLVER, POGMOOR, 1930

I do not know whether Fury had anything against the dog or not, but he shot at it.

One of the most extraordinary cases to come before magistrates at Barnsley Borough Police Court for a considerable time was heard on Monday 23 June 1930. Fred Fury, a miner, of no fixed abode, was charged with being drunk in possession of a loaded revolver, not having a certificate for the firearm and ammunition, and with ill-treating a dog by shooting it.

The Chief Constable, Mr G H Butler, gave details of the offences, describing them as being very serious:

Fury was in Pogmoor Road about six-thirty last night. There was a dog in the road. I do not know whether Fury had anything against the dog or not, but he shot at it. He did not kill it, but caused a wound in its head, and the dog went yelping home. An hour later Fury was still in possession of the loaded revolver and ammunition. What might have happened if this man had run amok, being in possession of a loaded revolver, nobody knows...

Witnesses were called and they spoke of hearing the report of the single gunshot and of finding, afterwards, that the dog had been shot, the animal having been injured in the jaw.

Police Constable Mead said:

...Fury was drunk. He had sixty-seven rounds of ammunition and four were in the revolver...

Fury, in his own defence said:

It's right. Yes, and I fired the gun, but I did not shoot the dog.

Mr P St. John, the magistrate's clerk, addressed Fury, asking him the straight and simple question:

What have you got to say?

To which Fury replied:

Nothing sir.

The Chief Constable told the Bench that Fury had forty-four previous convictions, which prompted one of the Bench, T Fox, Esquire to ask:

Is he of sound mind?

To which the Chief Constable replied:

He is of very sound mind, sir.

The Chairman observed that Fury was placed in a very awkward position, but perhaps he did not realise it. He had shot a dog, and he might have shot someone else, not just the 'poor dumb animal'. For all three offences Fury was sentenced to six months' imprisonment.

FOWL STEALING AT LOW VALLEY, 1933

We thought we were getting something on the cheap.

On Friday 17 March 1933, three Monk Bretton men appeared before Barnsley magistrates on a charge of fowl stealing. Sixteen fowls, valued in total at £3, the property of Charles Coward, of Low Valley, were stolen on the night of Tuesday 28 February. The Bench heard that Edwin Sayles and John Sayles, both miners, and Hortis Bailey, a hawker, had colluded in order to steal the fowls. John Sayles and Hortis Bailey pleaded guilty and Edwin Sayles pleaded not guilty.

Police Inspector Spiers said that on the evening of Tuesday 28 February, Mr Coward had left his hen pen secure, but at nine o'clock the following morning he found that the fowls were missing. The police made enquiries, which revealed that the three defendants had been seen in the district with a flat cart and fifteen of the fowls, all hens, were found in their possession, on 8 March, the sixteenth, a cockerel, having been killed and eaten. It was assumed that Edwin Sayles had pleaded not guilty because he had only held the horse while the other two actually stole the fowls.

Police Constable Cooper said that, on being charged, one of the men had said:

I knew what it meant and I was a fool to take them.

Another said:

We thought we were getting something on the cheap.

In mitigation, the defendants pleaded that they had yielded to 'a sudden temptation'. The chairman, Alderman Herbert Smith, pointed out that Bailey had three previous convictions for theft and one of the others appeared to be following in his footsteps and to this man, John Sayles, Alderman Smith said he wished to give a warning and fined him 20s. and costs. Edwin Sayles, his brother, was fined 10s. and Hortis Bailey was sent to prison for three months. On hearing this sentence, a young lady collapsed in court and it was necessary to assist her outside.

CHAPTER 6

Concerning Children

INDECENT ASSAULT, WILSON'S PIECE, BARNSLEY, FEBRUARY, 1857

...after giving Mary a thorough examination, he advised that something serious had taken place.

On Monday 16 March 1857, considerable interest was shown as the courtroom listened to the serious charge brought against an elderly man named Thomas Yates, who appeared in custody at Barnsley courthouse, before Thomas Taylor, Esquire. Yates who had been arrested at the instigation of Henry Priestley on the previous Friday, was charged with committing rape on Priestley's twelve-year old daughter, Mary. The court heard that the offence had been committed on 15 February, but did not come to light until 6 March. On that day, Mr Priestley noticed that his daughter was in no small degree of distress. In fact she could scarcely walk. When he asked her what was the matter, she admitted that Yates had taken liberties with her and this had resulted in her present condition.

The court further heard that Mr Priestley took his daughter to Dr Smith. After examining the girl Dr Smith said he believed a rape had been attempted, but could not say positively that it had been effected. The girl was also suffering from a serious complaint as a result of the prisoner's connection with her. Priestley said that Dr Smith had advised him to say nothing about the matter. Not entirely satisfied with the result of Dr Smith's examination, Priestley took his daughter to see a surgeon, Mr Sadler, who, after giving Mary a thorough examination, advised him that it was his opinion that something serious had taken place. However, it was not until Friday 13 March that Henry Priestley brought the charge against Yates, which resulted in his arrest. Following developments since Yates's arrest the court learned that Priestley now wished to withdraw the charge, as a compromise had been attempted. The prisoner's friends had apparently agreed to pay the medical expenses incurred and also to allow the father a sum of money until the child got better. This information did not satisfy the Bench that the charge should be dismissed and the case was remanded until Wednesday, when it was further remanded. Following Yates being remanded several times more he made his final appearance at Barnsley courthouse on Wednesday 25 March, when he was brought up on a charge laid under the Aggravated Assault Act of committing an indecent assault on a twelve-year-old girl.

Mary Priestley of Wilson's Piece, Barnsley, said that on 15 February she went into Thomas Yates's house a little before teatime. He was alone in the house. He told her to come in and sit down. She then described what followed, clearly showing that Yates had behaved in a disgusting manner towards her. She felt very ill after Yates had finished with her and could scarcely sit on her chair. She said she did not tell her mother until about three weeks had elapsed.

In giving his evidence, Dr Smith told the court that he had examined the girl and found that there was something the matter with her, but there was no appearance of a rape having been attempted. Dr Smith added that he had also examined the prisoner, whom he found free of any complaint. He said he had had a conversation with Priestley about settling the matter, and that he seemed very desirous and urgent to make money out of the affair, stating that he would take £3 to settle it. Dr Smith added that he thought that if a sufficient sum of money had been forthcoming it would never have been brought into court. He said he had advised Priestley to settle the matter, as he considered it a very trumpery affair, got up to extort money.

Henry Priestley said that, following what his daughter had told his wife and himself about three weeks after the offence had been committed, he confronted Yates and charged him with it. He told Yates that he must either pay all the expenses or he should prosecute him. Priestley said Yates promised to pay all the expenses relating to his daughter's illness. Dr Smith also advised him to settle it. Mr Priestley said that he had signed a paper agreeing to withdraw the charge, but not before he had been approached by Yates's son who told him he could get his father off for £5. He added that he had received a sum of money towards compromising the matter. Charlotte Priestley, the girl's mother, simply corroborated her husband's evidence regarding Mary, informing them of Yates's conduct towards her. She added nothing further.

The defence produced an agreement showing that Henry Priestley had agreed to settle the matter for a sum of money effectively taking the matter out of the hands of the magistrates. This did not prevent them intervening at least in part. The Bench held a short conversation after which the chairman, J S Stanhope, Esquire, committed Yates to three months' hard labour at Wakefield House of Correction.

YOUNG BRUSH THIEVES SENT TO PRISON, BARNSLEY, 1865

...when he was packing his goods away, he noticed several other items had been stolen.

On Monday 14 August 1865, a group of boys between twelve and fifteen years of age were brought up in the dock before the Rev H B Cooke at Barnsley courthouse. Charles Lucas, the brothers Henry and John Thompson, James Richardson, William Shirt, William Frost, Peter Donagh, Charles Cherry, John Kilbride and Thomas Riley, were charged with stealing a quantity of brushes, on Saturday 12 August, the property of

Issac Mellor. Mr Mellor was the proprietor of a brush shop in May Day Green, and on Saturday night he had a stall in the market, on which were a variety of articles displayed for sale. At about ten o'clock, he noticed eight clothes brushes had been stolen from the stall. At the close of the market, when he was packing his goods away, he noticed several other items had been stolen. The cost of the stolen goods amounted to £2. He reported the theft to police and their enquiries led them to the house of the Thompson brothers, where officers were admitted by the boys' parents. Eight stolen brushes were found there, and it was also discovered that several other stolen items had been sold to various individuals. Evidence was produced which implicated all ten boys in the theft and all were found culpable and committed to Wakefield for seven days' imprisonment.

INDECENT ASSAULT ON A SEVEN-YEAR-OLD GIRL, WOMBWELL 1875

...gave the others some money to go away and when Sarah was alone with him, it was then that the assault took place.

On Monday 5 July, labourer Joseph Davison, was brought before magistrates E Newman, Esquire and F Taylor, Esquire, at Barnsley Town Hall, charged with indecently assaulting a little girl named Sarah Elizabeth Peas, aged seven, at Wombwell, on the previous afternoon. The Bench heard that the little girl was in the waiting room at the railway station with some playmates. Davison, who was alone there with the children, gave the others some money to go away and when Sarah was alone with him, it was then that the assault took place. He was caught in the act by other passengers, who prevented his escape, and he was promptly arrested by police. Davison was sentenced to two months' imprisonment, with hard labour.

INDECENT ASSAULT ON THIRTEEN-YEAR-OLD GIRL, DARTON, 1900

...pleaded guilty to a charge of committing and indecent assault.

On Saturday 16 March 1901, sixty-year-old labourer Henry Dawson, of Darton, was tried at Leeds Assizes, before Mr Justice Kennedy. He pleaded guilty to a charge of committing an indecent assault on a thirteen-year-old girl at Darton on 28 November 1900 and on other days. Dawson was sentenced to twelve months' imprisonment with hard labour.

WORSBROUGH BRIDGE PARENTS SENT TO GAOL FOR NEGLECTING THEIR CHILDREN, 1916

...two sons who were working and two younger sons all slept in one bed in which there was scarcely a dry patch.

On Monday 17 January 1916, a married couple from Worsbrough Bridge, colliery labourer Alfred Turton and his wife, Betsy, were in the dock at Barnsley West Riding Court, charged with neglecting their four younger children, aged fifteen, thirteen, eleven and seven, respectively. The Bench was chaired by G H Norton, Esquire. Also sitting were Alderman Rose and W L Wadsworth, Esquire.

Police Constable Hyde said that on 12 January, accompanied by Sergeant Brown, he had visited the defendant's house, which was in a filthy and neglected condition. The children were also in a neglected condition. Not only were they verminous, but they were suffering with sore heads and were all without exception, badly clad. The youngest boy, eleven-year-old Willie, was very emaciated and weighed only 3*st.* 9*lbs.* He was nothing but skin and bone, and every bone in his body could be seen protruding through his thin skin.

Constable Hyde then went on to describe the conditions in which the Turton family were living. He said the living room was badly furnished and very dirty, and there was only a bucketful of coal in the entire house. In the sparsely furnished front bedroom, there was an iron bedstead and two straw mattresses, which were in a filthy condition. There was no bedding in any of the three bedrooms and there was an appalling stench. Sergeant Brown corroborated Constable Hyde's evidence and Dr Beverly gave evidence concerning the condition of the children's health.

Evidence was then provided concerning the Turton family's finances. Alfred Turton's weekly wage averaged 35s. With the money contributed to the weekly budget by the Turtons two eldest sons the defendants had £3.10s. 0d. coming in each week. The rent amounted to 4s. 6d a week, leaving the not inconsiderable sum of £3. 5s. 6d. a week with which to run the household. During the evidence it transpired that Alfred Turton worked regularly but was a heavy drinker at weekends. However, Betsy Turton was said to be continually under the influence of drink.

Dr Beverley said that the defendants' son, Willie, weighed 1½ stones less than could be reasonably expected and that he was satisfied that the boy's condition arose from a state of semi-starvation. Mr J K Lee, for the defence, cross-examined the doctor and said he believed Willie Turton to be suffering from tubercular peritonitis, which would account for his condition. However, Dr Beverley disputed this. The doctor went on to say that two sons who were working and two younger sons, all slept in one bed in which there was scarcely a dry patch. The bed in which the defendants slept was verminous. Dr Beverley concluded his evidence by saying that the condition of the children was entirely due to neglect.

Mr Lee then called two of the older children to give evidence. Jack Turton, aged nineteen and Martha Jane Turton, aged fifteen, in their evidence both maintained they had plenty of food and clothing, and that the dirty condition of the younger children was as a result of them playing with children from other families. They had attended school regularly, with the exception of Willie, who had been ill for the last eighteen months, and couldn't keep his food down. Mr Lee then produced Willie and his younger sister and handed in a certificate from Dr Fryer, which stated that Willie was suffering from tubercular peritonitis. He then went on to say that the police evidence was mainly concerned with the dirty state of the children and the weakness of the boy Willie; and with regard to Willie, the certificate from Dr Fryer showed the boy was suffering from a type of consumption. Mr Lee concluded by saying that most of the children were old enough to keep themselves clean. Only one child was ailing, although they were all doubtless rough and ready. The only offence the defendants had committed was that they had been too generous to their children and had allowed them to have too much of their own way.

The Bench, however, were apparently unmoved and unconvinced by the proffered defence. After some discussion, the chairman, Mr Norton, said:

This is a very bad case, indeed; it is certainly the worst I have had before me in my experience. Instead of keeping your children clean, you treated them more like savages than anything else. The condition of the house is absolutely disgusting. You have been convicted before for similar offences – in 1905 one month, and in 1911 one month. Apparently it has not had any effect. There is no excuse for dirt, and you were earning good wages. We cannot give you less than three months' imprisonment.

As the sentence was being passed, a considerable din emanated from within the courtroom. Alfred and Betsy Turton's children were all present, including a married daughter and a grown-up daughter and son. Without exception, from the youngest to the eldest sibling, they all burst into loud crying and sobbing.

FINED FOR RIDING BEHIND TRAMCARS, 1916

... one boy had been killed and another injured.

An eleven-year-old Worsbrough Bridge boy, James Tordoff, found himself in the dock at Barnsley West Riding Court, on Wednesday 19 January 1916, charged with indulging in the dangerous practice of riding on the back of tramcars. Mr J

Raley, prosecuting on behalf of the Barnsley Traction Company, said this was the first case of its kind to be brought by the company and it was fervently hoped that there would be no further necessity for proceedings. Concern was expressed about mischievous children, jumping on the back of tramcars, and whilst holding the rail, riding considerable distances. The court heard that as a result of this practice one boy had been killed and another injured. In wartime Britain, since it had become necessary to employ lady conductors on the cars youngsters had been taking advantage in order to indulge in what they considered to be great fun. In the case in question, young James Tordoff had only been prevented from serious injury by the timely intervention of a police constable, who caught the boy as he released his hold of the rail and fell. To emphasise the seriousness of the case and in the hope it would deter others, the youngster was given a fine of 10*s*.

SERIOUS ACCIDENT AVERTED AS TWO YOUNG BOYS ARE THWARTED IMITATING THE PICTURES, SUMMER LANE, BARNSLEY 1920

…had the wheel of the engine run over the timber the engine would certainly have been upset.

Barnsley Borough magistrates were alarmed by what they heard when two local boys aged twelve and eleven years respectively, were brought before them, on Thursday 6 May 1920. The youngsters both pleaded guilty to maliciously placing timber upon the Great Western Railway, with intent to obstruct engines and carriages, on 16 April.

Both boys attended Keir Street School, situated only a short distance from Summer Lane Railway Station. Mr T Whitehouse for the railway company, said it appeared that after school hours the boys got onto the embankment and placed a piece of timber across the metal rails and a lot of stones on the line. Fortunately, the obstruction was found before any harm could be done and later, when he visited the school, the boys admitted their guilt. The only reason the boys could give for their conduct was that they wanted to see the engine jump. Apparently, after the boys had placed the obstructions on the line they left the embankment and went to Summer Lane Railway Station to watch a train go down the track. The engine ran over the stones but not over the timber, which had fortunately been removed. Mr Whitehouse said at the spot where the obstruction had been placed there was a falling gradient and a very sharp curve, and had the wheel of the engine run over the timber, the engine would certainly have been upset. Mr Whitehouse added that although the school was near the railway line this was the first time any boys had had to be brought to Court. When the magistrates' clerk asked the boys where they had seen such a thing done, their reply astonished the courtroom, when they exclaimed 'at the pictures!'

The parents of both boys said they had thrashed their sons when they had learned of the incident and the boys assured the Bench they would not offend again. Chairman of the Bench, Councillor England, while expressing regret that the Bench could not order the boys to be whipped, bound them over for six months, with payment of costs, the parents to be surety for their good behaviour.

JUMP SCHOOLBOYS' GRUESOME FIND AT WOMBWELL, 1923

...both arms had been destroyed, and half the right leg had been burnt off.

On 3 March 1923, the *Barnsley Independent* reported that an inquest had been held the previous Wednesday at the *Clothiers' Arms*, Elsecar, before the Coroner, C J Haworth, Esquire, the purpose of which was to investigate the finding by two schoolboys of the body of a newly-born male child. Thirteen-year-old William James Hopkinson, of New Buildings, Cemetery Road, Jump, said that on the previous Sunday, he and another boy, Joseph Whitehead, were out walking. As they were crossing Five Fields footpath, leading from Jump to Wombell Main, they came across a brown paper parcel lying near the path. On further investigation, they noticed what was

Dr Barclay Wiggins (1867–1959) (left) with his dog, Molly, and his son, Dr Albert William Barclay Wiggins (1903–85), at his home, Thistle House, Hoyland. Dr Wiggins conducted the post-mortem on the abandoned dead baby, discovered at Wombwell by two schoolboys. Mary Dickerson collection

clearly a human head protruding from the wrapping. The boys immediately went to report their findings to the police. Police Constable Parry said, having examined the parcel, he looked around and found the lower portion of the body, twenty yards from the head, over a wall, some three yards from the footpath

Dr Barclay Wiggins said that death appeared to have taken place about a week previous to the body having been found. The child's head was burnt, both arms had been destroyed, and half the right leg had been burnt off. The remains were generally charred and the heart had been completely destroyed in the burning process. Dr Wiggins added that there was no evidence that the child had had a separate existence.

Coroner: *It is very evident it had been on the fire.*
Dr Wiggins *Yes, as a matter of fact, adhering to the body was a burned piece of wood.*

The coroner recorded a verdict of 'found dead,' and added there was no evidence that the child had had a separate existence. It could only be assumed that an unfortunate young woman or girl had given birth to a stillborn child, and possibly having managed to conceal her pregnancy thus far, for whatever reason, in her efforts to continue the subterfuge, she had unsuccessfully attempted to destroy the evidence.

STARVING INFANT RESORTS TO CHEWING CARDBOARD AND CURTAINS, NEW LODGE, FEBRUARY, 1953

... the mother was able to borrow some bread and jam from the neighbours, but the next morning the girl went to school without any food at all.

In the aftermath of World War Two, during the period when food rationing was still in force, careful budgeting and the proper planning of meals was essential. However, when money was in short supply, many families suffered great hardship. Often food depravation was avoidable, particularly for those families whose breadwinners were not work-shy, but for others who apparently felt no obligation to provide for their dependents, there was many a sad story to be told, as shown by this particular case. In February 1953 a thirty-two-year-old miner and father of three young children was sent to prison for two months by Barnsley Borough magistrates, for wilfully neglecting children, in a manner likely to cause unnecessary suffering. Following Barnsley magistrates having heard the case, the Chairman of the Bench, Mr E H Umbers, described it as 'disgraceful and inhuman'.

The father, of New Lodge Crescent, New Lodge Estate, pleaded not guilty to the offence with which he was charged. The case was brought to the attention of the local Inspector of the NSPCC by the police, who had been alerted that something was amiss in the household by concerned neighbours. When police visited the house, a six-year-old female had arrived home from school. They noticed that the little girl picked up a piece of cardboard and commenced eating it. She forced the cardboard into her mouth and swallowed pieces of it. When the cardboard was taken away from her, she ran to the window and began to gnaw at the curtains.

When police officers asked the child's mother what food there was in the house, they were told there was a little flour and half a swede. The police officers then went to some neighbouring houses and returned with bread and other provisions for the family.

Mr J S Puddephatt, in opening the case for the prosecution described the circumstances to be revealed as 'absolutely shocking'. Mr Puddephat said that on Friday 20 January the mother had received just 18s. from her husband because he had only worked one shift during the preceding week. As she already owed £3 11s. for groceries, she was unable to obtain any further rations. However, when the defendant had been questioned, he said he could not help the situation. He had made no approach to the National Assistance Board. Mr Puddephatt went on to say:

The most callous feature of the case is that when the defendant knew that there was no food in the house he went to his mother's house for his meals...On the day previous to the visit by the police, all the family, mother and three young children had to eat was a little flour, half a swede and one potato. The potato was used to provide chips for the daughter. When she came home that night the mother was able to borrow some bread and jam from the neighbours, but the next morning the girl went to school without any food at all. The husband made no attempt to provide his wife with money to look after the children and to obtain rations for the family. He was not bothered at all about the family...

The mother said she married in February 1946. Her husband was not a regular worker and he kept leaving her. When she had asked him for money with which to buy rations he had told her that he could not help. During cross-examination she agreed that she had seen her daughter chewing at the curtains on a previous occasion and had asked her to stop, at which point her husband called out to her from the dock:

How many fights have we had over the kiddies eating their plastic dolls?

The husband then declared that there was no point in asking questions because his wife was lying.

Detective Constable Thatcher said that, after visiting the family house, he had immediately gone to the nearby home of a policeman and returned with half a loaf of bread, which he gave to the mother and told her to cut it into three portions. D C Thatcher added:

When she was given a slice of bread she devoured it like an animal.

NSPCC Inspector William A H Rawlings, of Pollitt Street, Barnsley, said that when the father was told the facts of the case would be reported, he replied:

I am not worried. I am prepared for a shock. I have been down before ...

Inspector Rawlings went on to say that the family's home was untidy. The defendant never went to bed. On the occasions when he worked, he returned home and slept on a couch in front of the fire in his pit dirt, with a filthy old blanked thrown over him. The bedroom was dirty but it seemed the mother hadn't the heart to keep the house clean.

In his own evidence, the husband said that the neglect of the children was not his fault. He had been separated from his wife and had only returned to her for the sake of the children. He went on to say:

I could have had a divorce and just paid money for the children but I went back to her and got a house for her and the children ... My wife can't cook. The family were living on the frying pan for every meal ...

Mrs 'F', a woman who was lodging at the family's house, was called as a witness in support of the defendant's claim that he had given his wife money to buy food for the children. She was prompted to remark that she must be careful what she said, as if she said anything offensive to the defendant, she might be turned out of the house and she could not get anywhere else to live. The Bench could find no mitigating circumstances and the husband was duly handed down a prison sentence.

CHAPTER 7

Suicides

DROWNING TRAGEDY OF ESTRANGED BRAMPTON BIERLOW WOMAN, HEMINGFIELD, 1892

…gave the girl a hat and an umbrella, saying that she was going to drown herself…

Thirty-nine-year-old Mary Ann Eccles and her husband Joseph, a collier, had been living apart since 2 May 1892, when Joseph had sold up their home, at Willow Green, Brampton Bierlow and turned his wife out. This separation came about because the couple had been living together, very unhappily, for some time owing to Mary Ann's drinking habits. Mary Ann then went to live at the house of Mr and Mrs Eyre at Concrete Cottages, where she remained until Saturday 14 May. On that afternoon a girl named Amy Atmoor, noticed that Mrs Eccles was very low-spirited. They had a conversation, during which Mrs Eccles gave the girl a hat and an umbrella, saying that she was going to drown herself, as the girl left Mrs Eccles began to cry. The girl said she wanted to walk with her but Mrs Eccles would not allow this. At ten o'clock that night, a man named Benjamin Heppenstall was talking a walk along the canal bank when he heard a woman's screams coming from the water but he was unable to give any assistance owing to the darkness of the night. He reported what he had heard to police and dragging operations commenced next morning, as soon as light permitted, Mary Ann Eccles's body was found at two o'clock in the afternoon in the Dearne and Dove Canal, at Greenland, Hemingfield.

SAD DEATH OF A DELUDED AUNT FOUND HANGED, STAINBOROUGH, 1923

She was hanging by the neck in the stair well.

Luicilla Adamson, a fifty-three-year-old spinster, of Steeple Lodge, Stainborough, kept house for her father. On the morning of Thursday 11 January 1923, Miss Adamson's ten-year-old nephew, Lewis Swann, paid a visit and was unable to get into the cottage. When his grandfather came home that afternoon at 4.50pm, young Lewis was put through a bedroom window. The boy found his Aunt Lucilla dead. She was hanging by the neck in the stair well. The rope was attached to a hook in the landing ceiling.

An inquest was held at the cottage before District Coroner, C J Haworth, Esquire, the following day, where it was heard that Lucilla Adamson had been depressed for the past few weeks and had threatened to commit suicide. Farm labourer Benjamin Adamson, the deceased woman's father, said a work box had been placed on the sitting room table, and in it he found three letters, one addressed to himself, another to the deceased's nephew, Lewis and the third to the coroner. The first letter read:

Dear Dad,

Forgive all the trouble I caused you. I can't stand it any longer. I know my head is going. I cannot work nor wait on you as I ought to do. Don't blame Lewis for his bank money. I have had it. I lost all your money and my own as well. Nobody is to blame only me. Forgive me and forget poor Cecilia.

Poor Dad! I didn't want to leave you, but I was forced to go first or they would have taken me. The clubman has the book. Don't bury me. Use the money on yourself. You deserve to be better looked after. I can't do for Lewis. Poor little Lewis! I can't take him with me. You don't know nothing that I have had to bear. I can't stand it.

The second to the little boy read:

Dear little Lewis,

Be a good boy. Auntie is forced to leave you. I cannot take you with me. Love to you. You wanted to go where I went but I cannot take you.

Lucilla Adamson's final letter, which was addressed to the coroner read:

He has been a good father, Mr Coroner, don't blame anybody. It is my doing. Dad does not know the trouble I have had on my mind. My mind's going by suffering. I can't stand by and do nothing. I tried so hard but it is no use. If I don't go he will have more trouble. I am sorry to have to leave him, but it has to be. I have a lot of worry.

The deceased's nephew, Lewis Swann, despite his tender years, was also called as a witness. The poor boy had hardly been given time to get over the shock of finding his aunt's body in such a condition, let alone having to face the ordeal of being questioned in such circumstances. Lewis said that, in December, he withdrew £1 from the bank at his aunt's request. She did not say what she had spent it on. He said that she had said to him the previous week that he might not see her again.

The coroner said there was no doubt that the woman was suffering from delusions. A verdict of 'suicide during temporary insanity' was returned.

DODWORTH MAN CUTS HIS THROAT, POGMOOR, 1930

...*the dead man was lying between the railings and the railway line in a bent position, with his throat cut.*

William Pinder, a fifty-five-year-old colliery by-product worker, of 16 Holdroyd Yard, Dodworth, where he lodged with a miner, Arthur Gough, was found dead on the railway embankment, on Sunday 11 May 1930, by haulage hand Arthur England. Pinder's throat was cut and a closed clasp knife was found in his pocket.

The inquest was held at Barnsley Town Hall on Wednesday 14 May, by Coroner C J Haworth, Esquire. The deceased's man's landlord, Arthur Gough, said Pinder left his house at 2.15pm on Monday 5 May, saying he was going to spend an hour in the garden. Mr Gough said he expected him to come back in readiness to go to work on the night shift, but he never returned. This did not particularly worry Mr Gough as during April Pinder had left the house saying he was going to the club and didn't return for several days. On that occasion, when he did return, he said he had been staying at his daughter's house in Royston. Mr Gough said of his former tenant and friend:

> *He has been a man you can hardly fathom, he was a big romancer. He had never threatened to do anything to himself, as he had a good home and good work. He had not appeared to be his usual self since Easter. He had been gloomy and appeared to have something on his mind. He wasn't a heavy drinker and gambled just a little. He had recently been off work ill.*

When shown the clasp knife which had been found in the dead man's pocket, Gough identified it as Pinder's tobacco knife.

Arthur England, of Vincent's Place, Barnsley, said at 4.50pm he was walking to the Recreation Ground at Pogmoor, when he saw the body of a man lying on the bank top by the railway line. Mr England immediately went to inform the police. Police Constable Freeman said he arrived on the scene at

5.25pm, and saw the deceased lying on the railway embankment. The railings separating the path from the railway embankment were five feet high and the dead man was lying between the railings and the railway line in a bent position, with his throat cut. The body appeared to have been there for some time. Constable Freeman added:

> I looked for an implement and I found the knife in his left hand jacket pocket. It was shut up, partly covered with a handkerchief and covered with blood.

Dr E W Blackburn, who was called to the scene, and who later made a post-mortem examination, said there was a pool of blood nine feet from where the body was found. The man's leg was broken just above the ankle but there were no signs of foul play. Dr Blackburn said he conducted the post-mortem on Tuesday, stating:

> I am of the opinion that the man had been dead three days. There were several wounds on the throat and the windpipe was almost severed. The wounds could have been self-inflicted by the knife [produced], and it was possible for the man to place the knife in his pocket. The right leg was fractured three inches above the ankle. The cause of death was syncope and exhaustion caused by haemorrhage from the wounds and shock from the wounds, fracture and exposure. The deceased might have broken his ankle by stumbling after the wounds had been inflicted.

In reply to a question put to him by the deceased's son-in-law, Dr Blackburn said Mr Pinder could have placed the knife back in his pocket after the wounds had been inflicted and had he been attended to at the time his life might have been saved.

Coroner's officer, Detective Williams, said he had made enquiries but had found nothing that would indicate why the deceased should wish to take his own life and he was unable to throw any further light on the subject. Miner Harold Mallinson, of 14 Agnes Road said on 4 May, while he was doing a spot of gardening, he saw Pinder leaning over the Bridle Bridge at Pogmoor. Mr Mallinson added:

The man seemed to be a bit funny.

On 6 May, Mr Mallinson saw Pinder again, standing in the same spot between 4pm and 5pm. Pinder walked to each side of the bridge and looked over. On the following Thursday, 8 May, Pinder was again on the bridge, and according to Mr Mallinson, he appeared to look worried.

The deceased's daughter, Evelyn Pryde, of 26 West Street, Royston, said the only trouble her father had was ill-health. When he had gone missing from Darton in April, he had firstly stayed at her home and then gone to stay with friends at Ryhill. Mrs Pryde added that her father had not been in the habit of wandering, for the last four or five years but before that he often did so.

In the absence of a suicide, note and with no further evidence to suggest a reason for William Pinder having taken his own life, the jury returned a verdict that 'the deceased cut his throat but there was not sufficient evidence to show the state of his mind'.

HOYLAND CHEMIST'S DEATH BY POISONING, 1930

…it was revealed that Smith had been suffering from ill health for a long time and a stomach ulcer was the suspected cause.

Thirty-five-year-old Thomas Albert Smith lived at 4 Duke Street, Hoyland, and was employed as an assistant chemist by the Barnsley British Co-operative Society Limited, at their Hoyland branch in King Street. At 10.30am on Thursday 26 June 1930, he was found lying dead in the lavatory at the chemist's shop where he worked, by the manager, George Atkinson.

An inquest was held before District Coroner C J Haworth, Esquire, at Hoyland Town Hall, on Saturday 28 June. Evidence was given concerning the deceased chemist's state of health and it was revealed that Smith had been suffering from ill health for a long time and a stomach ulcer was the

The Barnsley British Co-operative Chemists shop, situated in King Street Hoyland, on the extreme right of the photograph, where assistant chemist Thomas Smith took his own life in the lavatory in 1930, seen here c.1958. Bradleys, the shop standing on the opposite corner of the street, at King Street's junction with Booth Street, was in 1930 Bott's pork butchers shop. George Hardy collection.

suspected cause. Smith's manager, George Atkinson said he had known the deceased for about sixteen months and for the past six weeks or so, he had been depressed owing to the suspected ulcer. Smith had been to Sheffield on the day before he died for an X-ray examination. No ulcer was evident on the X-ray, a fact which the radiologist was to have reported to Smith's doctor. On Thursday morning Mr Atkinson said he missed Smith about 9.55am and he found him lying dead on the lavatory floor at 10.30am.

Police surgeon, Dr James Herbert Fairclough, of Walderslade, King Street, Hoyland, said he had made a post-mortem examination and had found traces of poisoning in Smith's internal organs. These organs also smelt strongly of potassium cyanide.

The Rev Harold Augustus Crowther Alwyn, Vicar of St Andrew's Church, Hoyland, a friend of the deceased, said Smith had confided in him, which had left him with no doubt that his friend's mind was affected. The jury returned a verdict of 'suicide whilst of temporarily unsound mind'.

GUNSHOT SUICIDE OF DARFIELD FARMER, 1947

Mr Whitlam was sitting in an old rocking chair, with the gun barrel between his legs, with his neck against the barrel.

On Monday 22 September 1947, an inquest was held at Darfield, before Deputy District Coroner, S H B Gill, Esquire, concerning the death by shooting of a local farmer. At 11.10am on Saturday 22 September, sixty-three-year-old farmer, Frank Whitlam, of Salt Pie Farm, Darfield, was found shot dead in the harness room at his farm. Mr Whitlam was sitting in an old rocking chair, with the gun barrel between his legs, with his neck against the barrel. Mr Whitlam's body was discovered by his farm labourer, thirty-three-year-old Arthur Gascoyne, of Thompson Road, Wombwell, who immediately went to fetch Mr Whitlam's son, who lived in Pitt Street, Darfield, and, who was at the time of his father's death, greasing his car.

The deceased's wife, Mary, said, her husband had been unwell for two years. In May he had been admitted to a nursing home when he received some treatment to his eyes, which had been giving him trouble. He was in no way depressed when he went in to the nursing home and he appeared to be slightly better when he was discharged. Mrs Whitlam added, although her husband had been unable to work for some time, he was able to knock about. She said she knew of no financial troubles which might have been worrying her husband, then added:

In fact, he had no troubles I knew of, except just a fear of blindness.

Douglas Whitlam, the deceased's son, said, on the morning of his father's death he had driven him to Wombwell for a shave. He had last seen his father alive at 10.45am, when he was sitting in the harness room wiping his gun. Having been summoned back to the farm by Arthur Gascoyne, Mr Whitlam said, on going into the harness room and on seeing his father:

I lifted his head and thought he was dead.

When Mr Gill asked him if his father had left any notes, Mr Whitlam replied:

He left nothing!

Dr E W Etches said that Frank Whitlam was a patient of his. He had been suffering from a disease of the central nervous system, which caused him to be dizzy and to lose his sight. He last saw Mr Whitlam some weeks ago when he appeared to be depressed, owing to his chronic ill health.

When Arthur Gascoyne was asked if his employer had ever complained to him, he replied:

He kept saying he didn't know what to do about his sight, nor how he could go on.

Mr Gill recorded a verdict that 'death was due to gunshot wounds, self-inflicted while the balance of his mind was disturbed'.

ROYSTON MAN GASSES HIMSELF AS HIS FAMILY RETURNS FROM A HOLIDAY, 1952

There was a note on the kitchen table in her father's handwriting.

A fifty-nine-year-old Royston bridgemaster, of Midland Road, Royston, remained at home while his wife and daughter went on a fortnight's holiday on 9 August. He died in Barnsley Beckett Hospital on 27 August 1952, having intentionally turned on the gas tap in the kitchen at his home, and remaining in the room deliberately breathed in the noxious coal gas. His wife and daughter returned home on 23 August. When his daughter entered the house there was a smell of gas and she

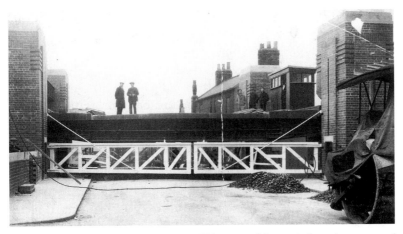

The bridge at Midland Road, Royston. This postcard image is from the camera of local photographer J L Wood. Brian Elliott collection

found her father unconscious in the kitchen. He was taken to hospital but died four days later. An inquest was held in Barnsley the following week before District Coroner, S H B Gill, Esquire.

An electric welder, son of the deceased, of Upper Castle Street, Bradford, said:

> *My father had complained of chest troubles since Christmas last year and had been under the doctor ... he was reasonably happy at home and I had never heard of any trouble between my mother and father and sister, apart from disagreements over small matters in the home. I know my father was worried about losing his job and house if the canal was closed down ... My father might have brooded about his troubles and magnified them while he was sitting alone in the house.*

The deceased's daughter said there had been differences in the home but only about small matters. On 9 August, she and her mother went on a fortnight's holiday, leaving her father alone in the house and had received a letter from him stating that everything was alright. Having enjoyed her two weeks' holiday, she returned home, only to find when she entered the house a strong smell of gas. She found her father in the kitchen, sitting in the armchair in an unconscious state. There was a note on the kitchen table in her father's handwriting.

The deceased man's widow said her husband was very quiet and moody and never seemed to take any interest in the home. Another witness, housewife, Mrs 'L', said she had spoken to the deceased on the day he gassed himself. On 23 August Mrs 'L' was out shopping. When she spoke to the deceased, he was standing on the doorstep of his home and he appeared to be quite cheerful.

Pathologist, Dr Lawrence Duggan, who made the post-mortem examination, said death was caused by hypostatic broncho-pneumonia due to cerebral haemorrhage and carbon monoxide poisoning was a predisposing cause.

The coroner, in conclusion, said:

The deceased was apparently a very morose man and had stated in the note that he was tired of home life and had clearly indicated that he intended to take his life.

The jury returned a verdict that 'he took his life while the balance of his mind was disturbed'.

DEPRESSED HOYLAND COMMON MAN DRANK ACID, 1953

...he was trying to get better and had said if he could not get better, he would be 'fed up'.

In 1953, a forty-nine-year-old single man who lived with his mother and brother, a labourer, at Stead Lane, Hoyland Common commited suicide. He had worked until 1937 at Barrow Colliery, when his head was split open in an accident, an injury for which he received compensation for a time. He was later given a light job. He collapsed at work in December 1952, and had not worked since. On Thursday 2 July, he took his own life by drinking sulphuric acid.

An inquest was held at Barnsley before the District Coroner S H B Gill, Esquire, on Tuesday 7 July. The dead man's sister, told the coroner that on Thursday 2 July she had breakfast with her brother at his home:

I can't say he had a lot of breakfast but he drank a lot of tea and smoked cigarettes. He washed up the breakfast pots and took my mother her breakfast upstairs. We sat talking until about quarter to eleven. He told me he had been to the pictures the previous night and said the Queen was on. I left him at home finishing washing up.

Mr Gill asked her about her brother's state of health, about which she replied:

He did not think he was getting any better ... I never heard him threaten to take his life ... I was called from home about 1.30pm the same day ... I found my mother screaming and Albert was on the rug – something was coming out of his mouth.

Mr Gill: *Did he say anything?*
Sister: *He said he still wanted to die.*
Mr Gill: *Did you see a bottle?*
Sister: *No. I was told he had drunk some acid.*
Mr Gill: *What did he say?*
Sister: *He said, 'I want to die...' Somebody sent for the doctor. The doctor asked what he had taken and I heard him say acid.*
Mr Gill: *Was any acid ever kept in the house?*
Sister: *No.*

The witness said she accompanied her brother to the hospital in the ambulance. He remained conscious throughout the journey, but he said nothing at all and died soon after he arrived at the hospital. She went on to say that her brother suffered from nerves and that he was trying to get better and had said if he could not get better, he would be 'fed up'. She added that her brother had no money worries.

Police Sergeant Harry Rhodes, stationed at Birdwell, was called to the family's house following the death. When he went to the dead man's bedroom, he found a medicine glass containing some dark liquid. The glass was produced and shown to the court. Sergeant Rhodes said there was no container that might have held the liquid, nor were there any messages or a suicide note. The sergeant concluded his evidence by saying:

I discovered that the deceased visited the works of Newton Chambers Ltd. on the night of June 30th. It is known he visited the fire station where sulphuric acid is kept. I took a sample from Newton Chambers and found it resembled the liquid in the glass.

The pathologist who carried out the post-mortem examination, Dr D E Price, said:

Death was due to sulphuric acid poisoning. The deceased probably suffered discomfort from gallstones and gall bladder trouble. There was no evidence of old head injuries. During my examination of the body, I found a scratch on the left breast. The scratch had no bearing on the man's death. He might have tried another method first.

The coroner recorded a verdict of 'death due to sulphuric acid poisoning self-administered while in a fit of depression about his health'.

CHAPTER 8

Manslaughter at Oxspring
July 1860

I'll give it thee...

An inquest was held at the *Waggon and Horses* inn, Oxspring, on Tuesday 24 July 1860, before Thomas Taylor, Esquire, in the absence of Thomas Badger, Esquire, coroner, on the body of Joseph Haigh, who was found lying dead, on the high road near Oxspring, at about half-past-eleven on the previous Sunday night. A farmer, Isaac Shore, was charged with manslaughter.

Labourer John Turner, employed at Fox's mills, Hunshelf, was the first witness to be called. He said he had known the deceased man for eight years. On the afternoon of Sunday 22 July he had met him at a cottage near Snowden Hill, known as Dyson's Cote, the home of Mr and Mrs Bentley. Turner said that between five and six o'clock he had met with Joseph Haigh at Dyson's Cote and they had afterwards adjourned to the *Waggon and Horses*, where they had a 'pint or two' of beer. Shortly after their arrival Isaac Shore turned up and Turner invited him to join their company. Turner said that neither Haigh nor Shore had any particular conversation, the chat being of a general nature. At about eleven o'clock, Turner told Haigh that he was going home, to which Haigh replied that he would follow him. Turner left the *Waggon and Horses* with a man named Dyson and went as far as Oxspring toll bar, where they stood for some time talking, during which Haigh and Shore turned up. Dyson parted company and Turner joined Haigh and Shore. Shore proposed that they go to the Bentley's cottage, which they did so, briefly, Turner taking the opportunity to light his pipe. After standing for a few minutes, they all walked away together. When they had walked about a hundred yards and passed under the railway bridge, Shore said to Haigh:

I'll give it thee for thy bad behaviour yet.

As he spoke these words, Shore gave Haigh a violent shove, knocking him to the ground. Haigh got up after a few moments and continued walking but Shore was insistent on continuing with the quarrel saying:

You're a damned lazy bugger, I cannot tell how you maintain your family.

To which remark Haigh asked Shore what he had done, and Shore replied:

I'll let thee see!

Then Shore put his fists up and struck Haigh a blow, which felled him. Turner got between the two men and Haigh got up and continued walking. Turner said:

We walked abreast, I being in the centre. We had not got many yards further when Shore placed himself in a threatening attitude, and I said I would not have any more of it.

Shore then threw off his coat, saying he would fight them both, to which Turner said that before he agreed to fight he must know what he was going to be fighting for, at which point Shore rushed past Turner and the next thing Turner heard was the sound of a heavy blow being struck and saw Shore and Haigh both going down together. Haigh appeared to fall heavily. Turner then went over to the men and insisted that Shore get up. Shore obliged and Turner continued to remonstrate with him. Meanwhile, Haigh was lying in the road with his head on the footpath. Turner attempted to assist Haigh to get up but Turner said Haigh appeared to have no use in himself. Shore said:

Leave him alone he's only shamming.

But Turner felt otherwise, replying:

No, I shan't leave him like this.

Having heard these words, Shore walked away. Turner said that on seeing Haigh in such a helpless condition and fearing that he might be dead, he hurried back to Dyson's Cote for help. The Bentleys and a neighbour, tailor John Ives and others returned with Turner and discovered Haigh was indeed dead. Mr Ives had already suspected this to be the case when he had come across Haigh lying in the road, just moments before, as he was returning home. He had rushed to the Bentley's and overheard Turner telling them what had happened. They lifted the lifeless Haigh off the road and carried his body to the *Waggon and Horses*, where they arrived at about 12.20am.

Mrs Mary Bentley said when the three men called at her cottage, following their being at the *Waggon and Horses*, they all appeared to have been drinking, but Shore was the worst. Mr Eyre, surgeon, of Barnsley, conducted a post-mortem examination of the body. He said:

Externally I found an abrasion on the right cheek, about an inch below the eye, and another about two inches above it. The former

A present-day view of the Waggon and Horses, *Oxspring.* The author

I should say might have been produced from a blow with the fist, the second more likely from a fall. I opened the head, and found the brain perfectly gorged with blood, evidently from the rupture of one of the larger blood vessels. Both ventricles were full of coagulated blood. The base of the brain was healthy. On descending to the spinal cord, I found that the atlas or the first bone of the neck was quite out; the second or axis bone was broken, and the ligature torn. I judge that the injuries sustained would be by forcibly striking the body back with such force as to project the head forwards, thus displacing the atlas from the axis. The pressure on the spinal cord would produce the appearances on the brain, and account for deceased never being able to speak or groan after he had fallen. The stomach and viscera were healthy.

Police Constable Whittaker gave evidence concerning Shore's admission. On the constable telling Shore that there was a serious charge against him, Shore replied:

Yes, it is, and I'll tell you all about it.

Constable Whittaker then told Shore:

You must consider yourself my prisoner, and anything you say to me may be used as evidence against you.

Shore then told Constable Whittaker:

After we left Bentley's cottage and got a piece on the road, I had an altercation with the deceased about a report he had published in reference to myself and a young woman at Snowden Hill. I shoved him down twice; and I believe I struck him once or twice; not oftener. When he was down I thought the deceased was shamming, and I went away and left him. I did not know he was dead until six o'clock the following morning.

Constable Whittaker continuing with his evidence, said:

During the time we were thus conversing, we came to the road where the body was found, and the prisoner said, 'This is the place.' I replied, 'Yes, there has been some scuffling here.' I forwarded the man to the police office at Barnsley, charged with manslaughter.

After a short consultation, the jury brought in a verdict of 'manslaughter' against Issac Shore. Shore remained silent as he was committed to take his trial under the coroner's warrant at the next assizes at York. Two farmers, George Green and George Brook, offered to stand bail on behalf of the prisoner. Bail was granted, each man paying a surety of £50.

On Wednesday 19 December, Shore appeared before Mr Justice Hill at the Yorkshire Winter Assizes on a charge of manslaughter. The jury found Shore guilty, but because of his excellent character, recommended him to mercy. His Lordship sentenced him to be imprisoned for two months, with hard labour.

CHAPTER 9

Brutal Slaying of a Woman at Barnsley
April 1868

You murdering villain, you'll kill her.

On Sunday 5 April 1868, a woman was brutally killed, in Court No 2, Joseph Street, Wilson's Piece, Barnsley. She was a widow and been living there for about three months with her nine-year-old-daughter and her common law husband, whom she had lived with for four years. The place they occupied was described as being wretchedly small, the entrance door being only five feet high. It consisted of just one room and was more like a hovel than a home.

The woman, Charlotte McReady (or Macready, as one account has it), was aged about thirty. The man, James Harris, a mason, was known locally as 'Scotty' or 'Scotch Jimmy', because he, like Charlotte, hailed from north of the border. According to neighbours, they lived very unhappily together and he had ill-treated her on several occasions. Harris had also developed a deep hatred for Charlotte's daughter, Ellen, and there were often quarrels over Charlotte's refusal to turn Ellen out of the house.

At a quarter to nine on Saturday evening Charlotte and Harris were drinking with two men named John Holdsworth and William Fox at the *Griffin Inn*. Holdsworth later said that Harris was already intoxicated and that Charlotte, although she had been drinking, was not drunk. The four then went to the *Dusty Miller* where they consumed a further two pints each. Harris then told Charlotte to go and buy something for supper. She left all three men near the *Neptune Inn*, which they went into. She returned a little later and they had three quarts of ale between them. She said she had bought some fish and, after drinking the ale, they all went back to Harris's house for supper and she cooked the fish. While the fish was cooking Charlotte went to the *Commercial Inn*, where she drank a glass of rum, in company with a neighbour, Mrs Hinchcliffe before returning home with half a gallon of ale in a jug, which according to Mrs Hinchcliffe, Charlotte had told her was for her husband. They all sat down at the table and ate the meal. Holdsworth and Fox left the house at about half past one. As they left, Harris lay down on the bed, he was swearing. John Holdsworth said later that the daughter was in the house when they were eating the fish but he did not notice her when he and Fox left. In fact the girl was trying to sleep. She said later that after the men had left, her mother and Harris quarrelled. She saw Harris strike her mother and was so frightened that she fled the house in case he beat her also. She spent the night with a neighbour named Sarah Havroe. At about twenty minutes to two, Charlotte left the house and went to visit an elderly neighbour in the same yard, Mary Galland, and she talked with her for a while. Charlotte asked Mrs Galland if she would return home with her. She did so and while Charlotte went to the bed to see if Harris was asleep, Mrs Galland waited at the threshold. Harris was fully clothed, laying across the bed with his feet towards the fire. Charlotte said:

He is asleep. I'll turn him over. Poor James, I'll loose your boots for ease for your feet.

As she began to unlace his boots Harris woke up in a rage and accused Charlotte of having robbed him, to which she replied:

James, it's your Charlotte that's gotten it, and you'll get it in the morning.

With that Harris got off the bedstead, doubled his fist, sprang at her and struck her on the temple, knocking her to the floor. He then kicked her three or four times on the right side, while she lay on the floor, all the time calling out abuse to her. Whereupon Mrs Galland seized hold of his coat lapels and said to him:

If she has your money you will get it in the morning.

Harris then began verbally abusing Mrs Galland, saying to her:

You old – I'll serve you the same.

Mrs Galland again took hold of his lapels and said to him:

You murdering villain, you'll kill her. I'll fetch a policeman.

To which Harris replied:

If you don't run out of here directly I'll do the same to you.

Harris then picked up a knife and ran at her. Mrs Galland fled from the house, as she did so, she held the door by the latch and said to Harris:

James, if she has the money, she has it down her dress.

As she appeared to leave the house Mrs Galland held the door by the sneck and watched what followed through the partially open door. Harris put his hand into Charlotte's dress and drew out a black purse, which he put into his pocket. He then resumed the attack on Charlotte, kicking her again in the face. At the third kick she called out:

Oh James, you have killed me!

Harris then drew his foot back and stamped on her temple, the sound that it made with his heavy boots, Mrs Galland could hear quite clearly. Mrs Galland then went in search of a policeman but couldn't find one. When she returned a short while later she listened at the door. Hearing no sound, she thought Harris and Charlotte had gone to bed, so she went home. Clearly satisfied with what he had done Harris, in the interim went back to the bed, lay down and slept. Nothing more was heard that night. The following morning John Wagstaffe, stone mason, of New Street, went to the house at about seven o'clock, to call on Harris to go out walking. He knocked on the door but received no reply. After about five minutes, Wagstaffe opened the still partially open door and went inside, where he found Charlotte McReady lying dead on the floor, with coagulated blood around her head and body. James Harris was lying asleep on the bed. Wagstaffe roused Harris, who upon been woken and questioned as to what had occurred, replied:

I've finished her at last. Whatever will become of me; what am I to do?

John Wagstaffe told Harris:

It's no use you running away Jimmy, they'll catch you wherever you go. You have had something to do with it because your boots are bloody.

Harris then got off the bed, picked up a cloth and wiped the blood off his boots. Wagstaffe then said:

Just stop. I will not be above a minute away.

Wagstaffe then went to summon help and told a neighbour Robert Flowers, about the dead woman. By the time Wagstaffe returned, Harris had gone. He had rushed out of the house without his cap and fled in the direction of Stairfoot and Ardsley. The police were summoned and Inspector Greenwood arrived, with other police officers, at about seven-thirty. The body was removed to the *Commercial Inn* and Inspector Greenwood, John Wagstaffe and some police officers went in pursuit of Harris, who was apprehended about two miles from Doncaster. When Inspector Greenwood arrested Harris and charged him with murder, Harris said:

I know about it … I found her drinking with two strange men in my house last night. I left them and when I came back again the men were gone, and she was laid on the floor, and [pointing to John Wagstaffe] *that's how Jack found her this morning.*

An inquest was held on Tuesday 7 April at the *Commercial Inn*, Wilson's Piece, Barnsley, before Thomas Taylor, Esquire, coroner. Several hundred people waited outside, hoping to get a glimpse of James Harris but the coroner said it was not necessary to produce him. The proceedings lasted almost five hours, from six in the evening until almost eleven o'clock.

Evidence concerning events leading up to Charlotte McReady's death was provided by several neighbours including, crucially, Mrs Mary Galland, as well as the victim's daughter, Ellen, John Holdsworth, stone mason, of Dodworth and Thomas Wainwright, surgeon, of Barnsley, who told the inquest:

I have made a post-mortem examination of the body. The deceased was a stranger to me. I first saw the body on Monday morning at the Commercial Inn. *Externally there was a wound above the orbit of the left eye, two inches in length and cut into the bone; another about the same length about half an inch below the eye; a very jagged lacerated wound on the same eye. On the same side of the head the forehead was much bruised. The right cheek was very much bruised and the right ear. There are no marks on the side of her body, but her clothes might prevent injury there. Internally the skull is fractured. Corresponding with the wound on the eye, there is a laceration of vessels underneath the scalp, but no fracture. The substance of the brain was healthy, but very much congested with blood; a fracture on the base of the skull. The vessels called Willis's arch were ruptured. From this cause death would be instantaneous. The lungs, heart and bowels were all healthy. My opinion is that death has been caused by fracture of the skull, with rupture of vessels causing effusion of blood on the brain. It might be produced from falling, but I am inclined to think it had been something of a very sudden and violent character such as a kick. A kick from the boots produced would be likely to cause such wounds as I have described. Deceased would be about thirty years of age.*

Witness evidence was very compelling and detailed. The coroner then summed up, during which he explained the law concerning murder. The coroner's jury, after an interval of three quarters of an hour, brought in a verdict 'that James Harris had murdered Charlotte McReady'.

On Thursday 9 April, James Harris was brought up at Barnsley Police Court charged with murder, before Rev H B  Cooke, T E Taylor, Esquire and E Newman, Esquire. During the hearing Harris stood in the dock appearing to treat the matter with the greatest indifference. As several witnesses gave their evidence Harris stood with both hands in his pockets. He was a man of relatively small stature, standing 5ft 3in tall, with auburn hair and a red flowing beard. The evidence was much the same as that given at the inquest. Towards the conclusion of proceedings, Harris said:

The witnesses have not said a word of truth; I was lying drunk in the house, and know nothing about it.

The chairman, Rev H B Cooke, concluded by saying:

It is my duty to commit you to the next assizes on a charge of wilful murder.

James Harris's trial was held at the Crown Court, Leeds Town Hall, during the Yorkshire Summer Assizes, on Monday 10

August, before Mr Justice Lush, indicted for the wilful murder of Charlotte McReady. Mr Vernon Blackburn and Mr Tenant prosecuted. Mr Bruce defended the prisoner.

Mr Blackburn opened the case for the prosecution by outlining the events leading up to and immediately following Charlotte Mc Ready's death, concluding his opening speech:

> *... In the morning, about seven o'clock, a man named Wagstaffe went to the house, and found the woman dead upon the ground, with the blood coagulated round her, and the prisoner on the bed. He asked the prisoner what he had done and he replied, 'I have finished her at last.' He then took a cloth, and wiped the blood off his boots, and said to Wagstaffe, 'What else can I do?' He told him that it was no use his trying to get away, because he would be captured, and the prisoner afterwards was apprehended at Doncaster. When charged with the offence, however, he gave another story, and said that he found two men drinking with her, that he left her with them, and when he returned he saw that she was dead, and that he had never touched her. That the brutal violence used by the prisoner caused the death of the deceased there can be no doubt, for it caused a fracture of the skull, and a tearing of the vessels at the base of the brain.*

Witnesses were than called and the full details of Harris's involvement in the death of Charlotte McReady was revealed to the courtroom. After hearing witness evidence and having put several questions during the course of it, Mr Bruce, for the defence pointed out:

> *... there is an entire absence of motive which might commend itself to any reasonable creature to wish to take away the life of Charlotte McReady, that the man was in such a condition that when suddenly awakened from sleep, he could not form any intention to kill her, and that he was devoid of any ability to form a desire to injure her. It is also clear that they had lived upon good terms; that he had done all for her comfort he could be expected to do. Besides, the prisoner had really in his hand a knife, a deadly weapon; but he did not use that, and it seems to me to be a strong proof of the absence of intention to kill. Although drunkenness is*

no excuse for crime, yet it is a proper subject to be looked upon by a jury when considering the question of premeditation and when you are deciding the point of murder or manslaughter, and it is for you [the jury] *to say whether the state of drunkenness in which the prisoner was, did not reduce the crime with which he was charged to that of manslaughter. Then the man had not gone away from the place, which would be the first action of a man who had committed murder, and under all these circumstances I submit that although the prisoner has committed a detestable and abominable outrage upon the woman, there is not sufficient evidence to find him guilty of murder.*

In summing up his Lordship said:

There is no doubt whatever that the death of the woman was due to the violence of the prisoner, and the only question for you [the jury] *to decide is whether the act was done under circumstances which made him guilty of murder, or whether there is anything in the circumstances which, by law, would reduce it down to the crime of manslaughter. It is my duty to tell you that it does not require any deliberation to make an act malicious in the legal sense, so as to make the party who did it guilty of murder. Any person who took away the life of another on a sudden impulse, without provocation, without justification, and without circumstances which the law admitted as palliative, was guilty of murder. The suddenness of the act did not reduce it. The question was, whether he did the act with violence, intentionally, and whether the act was such that the probable consequences would be to take away life. Therefore, the question which you will have to decide is whether he did the act intentionally, and whether having regard to the aim he made with his feet, the act he did was such as in the general, and under the circumstances, would probably take away the life of a fellow being; and if he did he would be guilty of murder. There is nothing in this case at all to show that the woman had provoked the prisoner so as upon that ground to reduce the crime to manslaughter. Upon the question of drunkenness it is my duty to tell you that an act is not palliated in the slightest degree of common law by reason of it being done under the influence of drunkenness. The law says that no person who committed the crime of drunkenness could claim indulgence for any wrongful act which he might do when in that condition. He could not by admitting one offence palliate it by another, and the law regarded him as equally responsible as a sober person. I invite you to consider whether the prisoner knew, when he gave the mortal wound, he was kicking at the woman's head. If he did kick at the head, the question is whether the blow he gave was such as any person would suppose would cause death.*

The jury retired to consider their verdict about one o'clock. Around seven o'clock in the evening they were summoned into court by the judge, as they were still undecided on a verdict. The judge asked if he could be of any assistance regarding any aspects of the evidence. His Lordship was informed that one particular juror had formed the opinion that if they brought in a verdict of manslaughter that the judge could only sentence the prisoner to two years' imprisonment. Mr Justice Lush clarified the situation by saying:

I can only tell you as a matter of law that we have, with regard to manslaughters, the widest range of sentences, from one hour's imprisonment to penal servitude for life.

The foreman of the jury then informed his Lordship:

I think, my Lord, we will now be able to arrive at a verdict.

The jury consulted for a few minutes in the jury box before the foreman told his Lordship that they had arrived at their verdict. They found the prisoner guilty of manslaughter.

Mr Justice Lush in passing sentence told Harris:

If the jury had found you guilty of murder, I should have had no alternative but to pass upon you, prisoner, the sentence of death. The jury, however, have found you guilty of manslaughter, which is not now a capital offence, but in which there is every shade of criminality, from the verge of murder down to the verge of justifiable homicide. Accepting the verdict of the jury, I feel that your crime, although not found by them to be murder, is the next approach to murder, and I should not be doing my duty if I did not sentence you to penal servitude for life.

The jury's verdict proved somewhat controversial and prompted several newspapers to comment on the case. The *Manchester Examiner and Times* reported:

> *Familiar as we unhappily are in this country with crimes of violence, few have ever equalled in sheer, unmitigated brutality the case of woman-killing at Barnsley, which was investigated on Monday at Leeds Assizes ... He knocked her to the earth with his fist, and then with his heavy boots, of which the poor soul had wished to relieve him, he kicked her as only such morose savages can, and a last, stamping his heel down into her temple, crushed the life out of her. A brutal case truly and without a solitary redeeming feature. One's soul instinctively shudders at its utter repulsiveness. And yet it seemed to baffle the comprehension of a Leeds jury. After an absence of six hours, during which the jury were unable to decide on their verdict ... One of the jurors was afraid that if they found the prisoner guilty of manslaughter only, the judge could not sentence him to more than two years' imprisonment. Having his doubts on this point dissipated, the juror quickly brought his mind into accord with that of his fellow jurors ...*

Taking the facts of this case into account, and considering the sheer brutality of the killing, I think it serves to highlight that being put on trial for one's life could be something of a lottery. In as much as the verdict was entirely dependent on the impression created in the minds of the jurors, or in some instances, a particular juror's timidity or beliefs. In certain cases some jurors would convict simply because they did not like the cut of a man's jib, irrespective of the evidence presented. Many an innocent man has gone to the gallows in such circumstances. In other cases, if a sufficient number of jurors were of the opinion that the death penalty should be avoided at all costs, a brutal killer could escape the justice he deserved by being convicted of a lesser charge. The latter would appear to apply in the case of James Harris. However,

Mr Justice Lush exercised his right to inflict the harshest possible sentence available to him on Harris for the crime of manslaughter. This judge's comment regarding manslaughter having every shade of criminality is very apt. Many a man's life has been decided by that gossamer thread dependent on a juror's interpretation of the law relating to the difference between murder and manslaughter.

CHAPTER 10

Fireworks Explosion Results in Manslaughter Verdict, Barnsley
October 1868

John took hold of the stick and was in the process of being raised out of the inferno that was slowly engulfing him, when the flesh peeled off his hands and he sank back into the flames, where he perished.

Thirty-seven-year-old George Norris was a hairdresser and perfumer; and also a fireworks manufacturer, with business premises and living quarters in Sheffield Road, Barnsley. His manufacturing plant was situated nearby, in Doncaster Road. The works consisted of three buildings, two of which were joined together, with the third standing alone. The workforce consisted mostly of young boys and girls, with just a few adults in attendance. In the lead up to Bonfire Night, Mr Norris's manufacturing plant was particularly busy, with his workforce, adults and children alike, working many extra hours, making fireworks and crackers from gunpowder which was delivered to the works in 50*lb.* barrels, which was then mixed with other components in the magazine. On the morning of Wednesday 7 October 1868, at about 6.52am, when thirteen of the workforce were at work, a tremendous explosion occurred in the detached building at the works, blowing the roof off and severely damaging the walls. The sound startled residents throughout the area, shaking houses and other buildings and blowing doors open as far away as Hoyle Mill, where residents at first thought yet another explosion had occurred at the Oaks Colliery, before the tell tale plume of smoke could be seen emanating from the direction of the fireworks manufactory in Barnsley's Doncaster Road. Fire was quick to take hold, as, excepting the detached building, which was constructed principally of brick, the other buildings

A local resident is startled, as the blast from the fireworks explosion blows his windows in at 6.52am on 7 October 1868. Author's collection

were of mostly wooden construction. One of these buildings contained a large quantity of paper, the other was used for making fireworks. The manufactory was divided into work and storage areas, referred to as sheds.

Within minutes, a crowd numbering several hundred people had gathered. The close proximity of such a dangerous works to the scores of tightly packed dwellings in that part of Barnsley, was later to raise more than an eyebrow or two by those in authority. As the local populace, and those working nearby flocked to the works they were confronted by the terrible sight of several of the children who worked in the factory screaming dreadfully, their clothes either blown or burnt off and all of them suffering from burns of varying degrees of severity. Mr Norris, who had arrived only moments before the explosion, was got out alive, although dreadfully injured. Onlookers saw that the flesh was hanging down from his hands. The foreman, William Elliott Bywater, was also alive, although it seemed obvious to those who bore witness to his terribly mangled body that the likelihood of the poor man

Damage caused to one of the buildings in Doncaster Road by the fireworks explosion at Mr Norris's works. Author's collection

remaining alive in that state for much longer, was remote. He had been blown between thirty and forty yards from the building in which he had been about his duties.

As the crowd continued to grow all the while the fire was raging and when it became known that there were combustible materials stored in nearby buildings, there were many willing hands to remove them to a place of safety, in an effort to prevent the fire from spreading. Several men risked their own lives when they rushed into the burning buildings to rescue the dead and the living. One poor little boy, John Watson, was alone in the corner of one of the blazing buildings, but sadly no one could get near him for the flames. A particularly brave fellow, cabinet maker, John Butler, at tremendous risk to his personal safety, scaled a wall of the burning building, and, with the aid of a long stick, attempted to rescue the terrified youngster. John took hold of the stick and was in the process of being raised out of the inferno that was slowly engulfing him, when the flesh peeled off his hands and he sank back into the flames, where he perished. The injured were removed from the premises as quickly as possible, some to their own homes, others to the Union Workhouse.

The *Barnsley Times* reported:

> *… The accident happened as we before stated at eight minutes to seven o'clock, but it was twenty minutes to eight before the town hose was connected with the fire plug close at hand, and all the time the flames were raging. A portion of this time the poor women and children were being, as a bystander expressed it, 'roasted alive'. It was the opinion of those present that if the hose had been brought in anything like a reasonable time, the fire might easily have been confined to the building in which it originated…*

If the arrival of the town hose was somewhat tardy, thankfully, medical help was quick to arrive on the scene. Surgeons, Mr Lancaster, Mr W T Y Smith, Mr Wainwright (senior), Mr Wainwright (junior), Mr Blackburn, Mr Sadler and Mr Francis J Butler, were soon followed by others to tend to the injured, who were also, for the most part, the dying.

By nine o'clock, the fire had been totally extinguished. In the immediate aftermath, the list of the dead comprised as follows: Maria Cooper, aged thirty-five, wife of colliery labourer, James Cooper, residing in Baker Street, Barnsley; Henry Howarth, aged twelve, of New Street; Mary Ann Evans, aged sixteen, of Sheffield Road; John Edward Watson, aged eleven, the son of joiner, John Watson, of Lindley's Yard, Sheffield Road, father and son having only been in the town a few days. The four bodies were placed in a nearby stable. One of the boys had the flesh completely burnt off his legs from the knees downwards, where all that remained was the charred bones. The other boy's injuries also presented a shocking sight. The flesh of the back part of the head had been completely burnt away, revealing the skull. The dead boy's limbs were contorted, being drawn in all directions. The bodies were subsequently removed to the *Union Inn* to await an inquest.

The death toll was quick to rise as the day progressed. An inquest was opened and adjourned that afternoon, before Coroner Thomas Taylor, Esquire at the *Union Inn*, Sheffield Road, kept by Mr Michael Deane. The jury comprised, Mr John Ostcliffe (foreman), Messrs. John Braime, Charles Chamberlain, Edwin Arthur Scholefield, Samuel Merryweather, Alfred Badger, Francis Johnson, John Lawrence, Joseph Woodruff, James Chipchase, John Hornby, George Brown, John Wilcock, William Sykes and William George Horsfall.

During this initial hearing, labourer Daniel Hawker, of Blucher Street, gave evidence concerning his fourteen-year-old daughter, Jane, who died, following injuries received in the explosion. Mr Hawker said, that Jane had been employed making fireworks for about two years. He added that he had seen his daughter shortly after the explosion, laid in a stable but still alive. She was taken home in an unconscious state, having been burnt all over her body. She was attended to by medical professionals but died later that morning. Mrs Hannah Lodge, of Racecommon Road, mother of twelve-year-old Sarah Ann Downing, who explained she had remarried following Sarah Ann's father's death, said, following the explosion she saw her daughter at the Workhouse at eight o'clock, alive and still able to talk. The dying little girl had said:

Mother lift me up and then I shall soon be with my father.

Sarah Ann died around noon. She was burnt all over her body, except for her feet, where her boots had given her some protection.

Hairdresser, Alfred Banks, said:

I live with Mr Norris and am his assistant. I used to assist in making fireworks in the morning. I have done this for three or four years, about two months in the year. I went into the manufactory about twenty minutes after six o'clock. I knew Maria Cooper. She did all kinds of work, she was not engaged in any particular department. I did not see any of the deceased before the explosion to my knowledge, except Maria Cooper. I first went into the far shed, where they finished the work, but I did not see who was there. The work appeared to be going on as usual. I then went into the middle shed, where the paper was stored … There was no powder, but some unfinished fireworks, containing a mixture. In the far shed there was a quantity of empty cases. It was in this shed that I heard the explosion. While I was there Betsy Hewitt came to me. She was then coming to work… I did not see Mr Norris at the works until after the accident. I saw him at home in bed, before it occurred. I saw him after the explosion at Charles Horbury's, a house close by. He was burnt very much … The girl Hewitt was not injured … I am not aware there are any precautionary directions or any printed rules by which the workpeople should proceed. I have never seen any other manufactory. I have been with Mr Norris about twelve years.

William Elliott Bywater, foreman of the works, aged thirty-six, of Waltham Street, succumbed to the serious injuries he had received in the explosion and died at 7.40pm on Thursday evening. George Norris, the works' proprietor, himself succumbed at 3.05am on Friday morning. By the time the inquest had been resumed on the following Tuesday eleven people had lost their lives as a result of the explosion, all but three of them children.

George Norris's funeral took place at the Baptist Chapel, situated in Sheffield Road at its junction with Britannia Street on the afternoon of Monday 12 October and was witnessed by a large number of spectators. The Rev John Compston officiated at what was described as an impressive funeral service and committal. The coffin was borne to the chapel by members of its congregation amongst whom Mr Norris had once numbered. He was afterwards laid to rest in Barnsley Cemetery. The bodies of the victims were also interred at Barnsley Cemetery in common graves at the expense of Mr Norris's estate, on various days, in the presence of thousands of spectators.

The resumed inquest was held on Tuesday 13 October at Barnsley courthouse on George Norris and ten others killed in the explosion. One witness, James Kaye, a joiner and builder, of Doncaster Road, said, on hearing the explosion:

I ran to the works and found them all in flames. I saw some of the persons employed running about in the flames. A person fetched a boy named Yates out. He was on fire, and I assisted to cut his clothes off. He cried, 'Oh Mr Kaye, rub my back.' I saw Mrs Cooper at the far end of No. 2 shed, near to where the stove was … I went to a cabin in which Mr Norris was and asked him how many there were in the ruins, and he said three or four. He appeared to be in great pain and said. 'Don't tease me.' On going back to the works I found them in flames. A hose was brought from Mr Savage's works in Doncaster Road, but it would not fit the hydrant … I then sent one of my joiners to fetch the hose from the courthouse. It was a quarter to eight before it could be got to work …

Caroline Robinson, of Copper Street, said she had worked at Mr Norris's fireworks manufactory for four years. She worked in the No. 4 shed making crackers and Elizabeth Hewitt, Sarah Ann Day and Mrs Cooper worked in the same place. They fetched the composition as they wanted it from the magazine and they were all at work until eleven o'clock on the night before the explosion. There was a lighted stove in the place where they worked. She said that she was so tired and weary from the extra work that she had not gone to work on the morning of the explosion, before adding:

Mrs Cooper used to put tins containing composition on the stove to dry. The tin used was a regular pudding tin, about 14ins. square. The last time I saw Mrs Cooper put anything over the stove was a few weeks ago …

Elizabeth Hewitt, a girl living in New Street, described how she had arrived at the works and had met Mr Norris. They had exchanged pleasantries and Mr Norris had then turned towards the left sheds and Miss Hewitt, the right. Miss Hewitt said, shortly afterwards, she saw Alfred Banks and as she was unfastening her shawl she heard a cracker go off, so she called out to Alfred to come. There were crackers flying about everywhere and she ran on the field, towards Measborough Dike, and came out at Horbury's house. Miss Hewitt said:

I ran to the house and saw smoke coming from the manufactory. Mr Norris came running up to the house. His clothes were in flames.

Druggist, Joseph F Johnson, of Cheapside, said:

I went to Mr George Norris's house, after he was injured. I saw him. He was in his bedroom, and was quite sensible. He said he believed he should not get better…He said, 'It is a bad job, but Mrs Cooper did it. She said when she got to the place this morning that the composition was too damp, it would not fill. She said she would put it on the stove if it blew the bloody place up.'

Mrs Elizabeth Horbury, of Doncaster Road, said:

I live near the fireworks manufactory. Shortly after the explosion Mr Norris came to my house, his clothes were on fire. I went to the door and called in two men that were passing, and they took his clothes off, and I put some blankets round him…Alfred Banks came to my house and said to Mr Norris, 'She had put it upon the stove,' and he replied, 'Hold your noise; and go and tell Miss Meade to get my room ready.' He offered up a very nice prayer, and appeared to be in great trouble. He was taken from my house in a cab.

Alfred Banks, hairdresser, of Sheffield Road, part-time assistant in the manufacture of fireworks, to the works' proprietor, Mr Norris, with whom he lived, again took the stand, as he had done at the initial hearing. He produced a plan of the works. During the course of his evidence, he said that when he went to the works on the morning of the explosion, Mrs Cooper had approached him with some composition (gunpowder mixed with other components to make crackers) in her hand, contained in a paper box or box lid, and had complained it was damp and would not fill. Meaning that, because it was damp, the powder would not flow into the cardboard tubes that formed the casing of the crackers and other fireworks. Mr Banks said:

... I was in No. 4 shed, and whilst there, Maria Cooper came in with a paper box, in which she had some composition, about a pound. She said, "My composition will not fill, and I will put it on the fire if it blows the place up." She then left, and in about three minutes the explosion went off. I did not take any steps for my own safety as I thought she was speaking in fun. Mr Norris and the foreman mixed the composition in a brick building apart from the manufactory shed. The children and the workpeople fetched it themselves as they required it ... The mixing shed is a building about sixty yards from the manufactory, and ten from the magazine. In the No. 1 shed there were a number of women and children, in No. 2 the foreman worked, No. 3 was stored with paper, and No. 4 I was in myself.

During his summing up the coroner told the jury that they:

... might also take into consideration the mode in which the buildings were erected, and if you think it proper you can recommend that in future no premises should be licensed unless the buildings or sheds are isolated. It seems almost certain that had such been the case at the works where this terrible explosion took place, that the deaths would have been fewer than they were. The first and principal person who you have before you is the woman Maria Cooper, who appears from the evidence to have had a knowledge of what she was doing, and if the other persons came to their deaths by her act, she would be guilty of manslaughter. If Mr Norris or Mr Bywater had seen her doing what the evidence said she did, and had sanctioned it, they would have been equally culpable, but this does not seem to have been the case ...

Having completed his summing up at 2.25pm, Mr Taylor directed the jury to retire and consider their verdict, which they did, after deliberating for a little over an hour. Mr Ostcliffe, the foreman, in delivering the verdict, said:

We are of the opinion George Norris, William Elliott Bywater, and others, came to their death by an explosion of fireworks at Barnsley, on 7th day of October 1868, and we are likewise of the opinion that the direct cause of death was the recklessness of

Maria Cooper in placing a tin of composition on the stove, whereby it exploded. We consequently return a verdict of manslaughter against Maria Cooper as to all parties dead, except herself. We are likewise of the opinion that children of such tender years ought not to be employed in such dangerous occupations. And the jury further say there appears to have been no proper regulations in conducting the works, and the sheds were unfit for carrying on such business.

The coroner duly recorded the jury's verdict.

CHAPTER 11

Lovers Gallagher and Swann and the Wombwell Murder
June 1903

Kick the bastard to death. Kick the bloody swine.

By the late evening of Saturday 6 June 1903 the word murder was on almost everyone's lips on the streets and in the taverns, inns and hotels throughout Wombwell, concerning a dreadful tragedy that had occurred earlier in the evening at a house in George Square (sometimes referred to as Alma Square), off George Street, situated in central Wombwell near the parish church, St Mary's. It soon became known that forty-four-year-old William Swann, a glassblower at Aldham Glass Works, had been brutally killed, following an argument with his former

lodger, John Gallagher, a labourer who worked at Mitchell Main. Tongues were also wagging about the relationship that existed between the dead man's wife and his supposed killer. The house where the tragedy occurred was within a hundred yards of the police station, yet, it was, however, to be a good hour and a half after the occurrence, before the police were informed.

Those who knew more of the backgrounds leading to the tragic

Mrs Edith Swann. Author's collection

events expressed no great surprise, for it appeared that life in the Swann household was not a happy one, as Mrs Swann was addicted to drink and possessed a violent temper. She had spent time in gaol having been convicted of a serious assault on a woman. The couple had separated on several occasions and recently John Gallagher had come to lodge with them. However, on being suspicious of his lodger's conduct towards his wife, William Swann had asked Gallagher to leave. Gallagher had then gone to lodge nearby with widow, Mary Ann Ward. Rumour had it that following the attack on her husband, Emily Swann, who was in a drunken condition, remained in the house with her injured husband; and as neighbours were used to the occasional fracas at the Swann's house, took no particular notice that anything seriously untoward had occurred, and as they were used to quarrels between William and Emily Swann, they considered it no business of theirs.

On this occasion, it appears that rumours were largely true. A little after eight o'clock Emily Swann seems to have realised that something was seriously wrong with her husband. She raised the alarm with neighbours and Dr Foley was sent for. The doctor was quick to arrive but it was clear to him after a short examination that Swann was dead and had been in that condition for about an hour. The police were sent for but owing to the drunken condition of the dead man's wife, were able to learn very little about what had actually occurred. Nobody else in the immediate vicinity, who were interviewed by police could throw any light on the subject. This gave Gallagher sufficient time to make his escape. Police Superintendent Quest was informed late on Saturday night of the events in Wombwell and at once made his way there.

On Sunday morning, police in all parts of Yorkshire and some further afield were informed of Gallagher's escape and a full description of the wanted man was given:

WANTED

John Gallagher

29 years of age
5*ft.* 7½ *ins*. high

Blue eyes of fresh complexion with dark brown hair and moustache. Tattooed on both arms, cross flags on the right upper arm and girls holding flowers on each forearm.

When last seen he was wearing a blue cloth jacket and vest, brown mixture cloth trousers, grey cloth cap, turned-down collar, and red and green spotted tie.

He is a native of Middlesbrough, and was discharged from the West Yorkshire Regiment recently for misconduct.

On the afternoon of Tuesday 9 June, an inquest was held before the coroner, Dossey Wightman, Esquire, at the *Three Horseshoes Hotel*, Wombwell. A large crowd had gathered outside the hotel and also in George Street, the greater portion of them being women. The assembling of the jury and their procession to view William Swann's body gave the crowd the signal that the inquest was about to commence and there were stirrings around George Street in anticipation of the widow leaving the house to attend. Great interest was expressed in seeing her by many in the crowd. The crowd were not to be disappointed. Shortly before the

John Gallagher. Author's collection

inquiry commenced Mrs Swann, accompanied by several relatives, left the house and walked down the street to the *Horseshoes Hotel*. She was recognised and acknowledged by a few of her neighbours, but for those who did not know her by sight her person quickly became known to them as a bandage covered her left eye. The police were present but the crowd, growing in number by degrees, and estimated to number a thousand strong by the time the inquest was underway, remained calm and not the slightest disturbance occurred. Once the proceedings began inside the hotel the crowd outside did not disperse. It seems they were determined to await Emily Swann's return. For that eventuality they were required to remain outside the hotel for about an hour and a half.

The jury comprised Messrs John Robinson (Clerk to Wombwell Urban District Council, who was appointed foreman), William E Swallow, James Nunn, Thomas Mackridge, F Diggles, William Muir, J B Ward, James Ogden, Thomas Fawcett, E Giles, Fred Wilson, Arthur Bamford and F Furniss. Police Superintendent A C Quest watched the proceedings.

The first witness was the widow of the deceased, Emily Swann. She stated that her husband came home at about a quarter to six on Saturday evening. She did not know where he had been, as he did not work on Saturday but he had not come home for his dinner. When her husband arrived at the house she was in the kitchen. The coroner then asked:

Who was with you?

Emily Swann:	*John Gallagher was coming downstairs when he came in. There was nobody else there then.*
Coroner:	*How long had he been there?*
Emily Swann:	*Not many minutes.*
Coroner:	*Did he lodge with you?*
Emily Swann:	*Not then. He had lodged with me.*
Coroner:	*What took place then?*
Emily Swann:	*My husband accused him of being with me.*
Coroner:	*What did your husband say?*
Emily Swann:	*He said I had been upstairs with him, that's what he said.*

Coroner:	*What did you say?*
Emily Swann:	*I never spoke.*
Coroner:	*Well, what took place?*
Emily Swann:	*My husband struck me on the eye.*
Coroner:	*What after that?*
Emily Swann:	*I got out of the house away from him, as soon as I could.*
Coroner:	*You ran out of the house?*
Emily Swann:	*Yes; I ran into Mrs Ward's, who lives across.*
Coroner:	*What then?*
Emily Swann:	*I said to Mrs Ward, "Look at my eye." John Gallager was in Mrs Ward's.*
Coroner:	*You showed him your eye?*
Emily Swann:	*I did not speak to him. I was showing Mrs Ward my eye. Gallagher said he would give it him, and ran out of the house.*
Coroner:	*You followed him?*
Emily Swann:	*Yes, and I told him it had nothing to do with him and he hadn't to go in. When he got in he struck him and started punching him.*
Coroner:	*Were they in the street then?*
Emily Swann:	*No, sir. My husband was in his own house.*
Coroner:	*Struck him where?*
Emily Swann:	*Struck him somewhere about the back of the neck, and then started punching him.*
Coroner:	*Did he knock him down?*
Emily Swann:	*Yes. He had him down and I tried to pull him off.*
Coroner:	*Where did he punch him?*
Emily Swann:	*Somewhere on his shoulders and on his head.*
Coroner:	*Once or many times?*
Emily Swann:	*It was a good many times, and when I tried to get my husband up he* [Gallagher] *struck me on the chin, and knocked me down.*
Coroner:	*Did you try to get Gallagher away from him?*
Emily Swann:	*I tried to pull Gallagher off, and he struck me.*

Mrs Swann then went on to describe how Gallagher's blow had felled her, she added that as she got up Gallagher was striking her husband with a wooden armchair. The chair was produced and Mrs Swann demonstrated by lifting the chair bodily and striking downwards with the legs to show what position the chair was in. She said she though Gallagher struck her husband with the chair legs more than once and afterwards banged the chair on top of the fender and then calling her husband a '——— bastard', with those word left the house.

Coroner:	*Did you go after him?*
Emily Swann:	*No. I lifted my husband into a chair and tried to give him some water, but he sluttered down out of the chair whilst drinking the water. I went to Mrs Ward's and I told her I thought Gallagher had very nearly killed my husband. She said she would not have anything to do with the matter. Gallagher was standing in front of Mr Beard's door. I said to Gallagher, "You have killed him; he is dying." Gallagher made some reply, but I could not tell what he said.*
Coroner:	*Have you seen him since then?*
Emily Swann:	*No, sir.*

Mrs Swann was then questioned by Superintendent Quest. During questioning she said that her husband had left home on Saturday morning at nine o'clock. When he returned home he was quite sober, as she was herself. When asked if she had had anything to drink that day she replied that she had a gill of beer. After again declaring that she was sober, she then added:

> *I was baffled because I was frightened.*

Following further questioning Mrs Swann said Gallagher lodged at the house for five weeks up to a month ago. Her husband told him to leave but she did not hear him give a reason for this.

Coroner:	*You know what it was about?*
Superintendent:	*Did your husband tell him to leave because of improper conduct?*

Where the inquest took place. Chris and Pearl Sharp of Old Barnsley

	Was he jealous because of intimacy between you and him?
Emily Swann:	*Yes.*
Superintendent:	*Did Gallagher afterwards come to your house?*
Emily Swann:	*Yes.*
Superintendent:	*Notwithstanding your huband had told him to go away? Had he been on previous occasions when your husband was out?*
Emily Swann:	*Yes, once or twice, and also when my husband was in.*
Superintendent:	*Have you ever heard Gallagher threaten your husband?*
Emily Swann:	*Yes.*
Superintendent:	*What has he said?*
Emily Swann:	*He said he would make him ready for a coffin.*
Superintendent:	*When did he say that?*
Emily Swann:	*Several times, he has told him so to his face.*

When asked why Gallagher had called at the house on Saturday, Mrs Swann said that he had called to collect some papers he had left there and also a pawn ticket. When she was asked what she knew about these papers Mrs Swann said she did not know he had left them, but when he came downstairs he had them in his hand. Superintendent Quest then turned to the events following her husband having arrived home and having seen Gallagher coming down the stairs. He asked Mrs Swann if when her husband had accused her of also being upstairs with Gallagher for an improper purpose; and if Gallagher had made any comment. Mrs Swann said that Gallagher had said something but she hadn't registered exactly what as her husband was talking at the same time. She also said that she did not particularly show Gallagher her eye, but he could see the injury her husband had inflicted on her. She said she could not get any help to her husband until the second time she went to Mrs Ward's, and her husband was then laid with his head against the cupboard door. There was only her six-year-old son and herself in the house part of the time when Gallagher was kicking her husband. She said she could not send for the doctor to attend to her husband until she had got somebody into the house and she did not know that Dr Foley was passing the house at the time.

Foreman of the jury, John Robinson, asked if it was in the past fortnight that Gallagher had made the threats against William Swann and the Coroner was able ascertain that these threats had first been made, following Gallagher having been asked to leave the house.

Dr George Ernest Atkins, of Wombwell, who made a post-mortem examination of the body said, there were several bruises on the right temple and cheek bone, the neck, and upper part of the chest, shoulders arms, and middle of the back. The covering of the brain was congested on both sides in the region of the temples, and the surface of the brain was also congested. On either side of the brain he found clots of blood. Death was due to effusion of blood into the substance of the brain, the injury being caused by violence. The breast bone was fractured, and the fourth, fifth, sixth and seventh ribs were also fractured on the right side. In all, Dr Atkins said he found about twenty bruises on the body, and great violence must have been used to cause them.

Widow Mary Ann Ward, said she lived opposite the Swanns, in the same square. Mrs Ward said that on Saturday when the tragedy occurred she had been drinking and was by no means sober. She added that Gallagher had also been drinking. In the afternoon Gallagher came to her house and sent her daughter to fetch his jacket and waistcoat out of pawn. Mrs Swann came to the house and took Gallagher's things to her house, although she was not sure of the exact time this occurred. Gallagher went out after her and brought his things back. Gallagher was a way just a few minutes and when he returned his said he would go and get washed. Shortly afterwards Mrs Swann came in and showed Gallagher her black eye. Mrs Ward said when Gallagher had asked who had done it, she replied, 'Mrs Swann's husband.' That was not long after Gallagher had come back. Mrs Swann had fetched Gallagher twice. After this Mrs Ward's evidence became a little hazy and she kept contradicting himself. A protracted tale of what was said and what was not then ensued until the coroner said:

Are you sure Mrs Swann asked him to come to her and give her husband something or do something at her husband?

Mary Ann Ward: *It was something of that sort.*
Coroner: *Do you mean it or not? Did Mrs Swann ask Gallagher to come with her to give her husband or do something at her husband?*
Mary Ann Ward: *I can't remember. I do not remember whether she did or not. I know she fetched him twice.*

Mrs Ward went on to say that she did not see Gallagher do anything and did not hear anything. Until Gallagher had gone she was not aware of the row that had taken place and of

Sheffield coroner Dossey Wightman, Esquire, (1836–1920) solicitor and partner in the Sheffield solicitors Wightman and Parker, coroner 1873–1911, who presided over the inquest. Author's collection.

Gallagher having done anything to William Swann. She afterwards saw the deceased laid out on the floor at his house. She said she later saw Gallagher at the *Royal Oak Inn*. During questioning by Superintendent Quest, Mrs Ward said that Gallagher was at her house most of Saturday afternoon and that Mrs Swann was quite sober. After Gallagher had been told that Swann was dead she had met him in the street but she did not know at what time. Gallagher asked her if she would have a drink with him and she went with him to Pashley's (*Royal Oak Inn*). She said the silly drink was in her head and she wished it had been far enough. During the time they were drinking at the *Royal Oak Inn* Gallagher never referred to the quarrel between himself and the deceased. She said she knew of quarrels having occurred before, she also knew Swann had been jealous and she knew Swann had ordered Gallagher to leave the house two or three times since Gallagher had given over lodging there. Only on Thursday Swann ordered Gallagher out of the house, who said he should only go for a better man. The husband threw a pot at his wife, which partly struck her. She knew Gallagher and Mrs Swann were together again that night. She had heard Gallagher say he would kill the bastard before he had done with him. When she told Gallagher that Swann was dead, he said something but she could not remember exactly what it was. It was something about serves him right, and he would give him some more to go to his grave with.

Another witness, pony driver Walt Wigglesworth, said he was a mate of Mrs Ward's son and was in Mrs Ward's house on Saturday afternoon, when Gallagher and Mrs Swann were having a drink together. They left the house together and about twenty minutes later Gallagher returned. When Mrs Swann returned, she had an injury to her eye and she said to Gallagher:

Look Johnny what our Bill has done.

Mr Wigglesworth said:

Gallagher went straight out followed by Mrs Swann who said, 'I hope he will punch him to death.'

Mr Wigglesworth remained at Mrs Ward's house and Gallagher returned about fifteen minutes later. He had some blood on his face. Gallagher said he had smashed him four ribs and he would smash the others before he went to Bradford that night. Gallagher then went to get washed. At about eight o'clock Mrs Swann came to the house and asked Mrs Ward if she would go and have a look at her husband as she was sure he was dead. Mr Wigglesworth said Mrs Ward didn't want to go but her son went instead. Later, Mr Wigglesworth saw Gallagher in the street and concerning Swann's death he heard Gallagher say:

I don't care.

Gallagher then proceeded to laugh and he started dancing and said he was not guilty. Mr Wigglesworth concluded his evidence by saying he knew nothing of the relationship between Gallagher and Mrs Swann, but he had heard of them going together.

Mr Wightman, in summing up said:

You have to decide how the man came to his death, and I think the medical evidence will satisfy you. Then you must decide if some person caused death and you must say whom. It is either murder or not. If the charge is to be reduced to manslaughter, this is not the place to do that. I cannot but express my doubts as to the reliability of the evidence proffered by Mrs Swann and Mrs Ward but it will still give you material to arrive at the point. If you believe Gallagher caused the man's death and I do not think you will have much difficulty with regard to that matter, it is your duty to send him for trial.

After a few minutes deliberation the jury returned a verdict of 'wilful murder' against John Gallagher. The foreman added that the jury wished to call attention to the fact that if Gallagher heard the remarks of Mrs Swann that she hoped he would punch her husband to death, whether the coroner should not consider her to some extent guilty in some shape or other.

Mr Wightman said that it was not a question for them to deal with. He was told, and not by the police, there was a considerable opinion in Wombwell that of the two, Mrs Swann and Gallagher, there was not a very great deal to pick between them. Still, that question was not before them. Nevertheless, the foreman of the jury desired it should be heard and Superintendent Quest said they would pay due attention to the point. For the purposes of the inquest the coroner recorded a verdict of wilful murder against John Gallagher. The proceedings having been concluded it was now necessary for Mrs Swann to return home. The crowd had steadfastly refused to disperse and had stood their ground. It was necessary for Mrs Swann's return home for the police to form an escort. As she left the hotel Mrs Swann was faced with loud jeering and hooting. However, the crowd restrained themselves and her police escort managed to get her home safely and the crowd on being satisfied they had made their feelings know, soon dispersed.

On Wednesday 10 June, the day of the murdered man's funeral, a crowd of several thousand people had gathered in the vicinity of Alma Square and George Street. Pockets of enraged citizens expressed their disapproval of the deceased man's widow, uttering threats of violence if she dared to show her head outside the door. Police Inspector Drury and Sergeant Minty were present with a strong force of constables. Among the crowd were many residents of Longcar, where Mrs Swann's mother was a resident. When the family mourners came out of the house there was a heavy swell as the multitude of onlookers clamoured to get a better look, hoping to see Mrs Swann, but she did not appear. It was later learned that police had persuaded the widow not to attend her husband's funeral. As the coffin was placed in a hearse to convey it to Wombwell Cemetery, the mourners followed on foot. The hearse was preceded by a contingent of workmen from the Aldham Glass Bottle Works, carrying what newspaper reports described as a beautiful wreath. The bearers were Messrs F Heppenstall, J Matthews, R Needham, J Chappel, J Goodwin, James Levitt, F Dale and J Oakland, all fellow workmen of the deceased. Mr Alfred Lightowler, manager of the works, was also present.

The service was conducted by the Rev R B Blakeney and only the relatives of the deceased were allowed inside the cemetery gates during the short service and internment. Family mourners comprised Mr Charles H Swann and Master Ernest Swann (sons of the deceased), Miss Helena Swann, Miss Annie Swann and Miss Swann (daughters of the deceased), Mr Alec Swann, Mr Tom Swann and Mr George Swann, of Stairfoot, all brothers of the deceased, and their wives.

On Saturday 20 June, the *Barnsley Independent* after reporting that Gallagher was still at large went on to say:

> *…It has been ascertained by the police that Gallagher, on the night of the tragedy, got away to Sheffield, and from there booked for Bradford on a midnight train but alighted at Manningham Station. Beyond that he has not been traced.*

In a lengthy article which involved a great deal of speculation as to Gallagher's whereabouts, the newspaper went on to say:

> *One of the most interesting incidents in connection with the affair is that Mrs Swann had prepared for a holiday on Friday last, but it is understood that immediately the police authorities were aware of her movements, they intervened, and Mrs Swann is still at home, going about in the ordinary manner. The children have been taken by members of the family to Barnsley and Bradford, the widow, therefore, living alone.*

Towards the end of the article, which had clearly been typeset during the course of the week it stated:

> *…It has since transpired that Mrs Swann has left the house occupied by her at the time of the tragedy, and is now living with an old widow lady in the same street, a few doors higher up.*

Early on the morning of Tuesday 4 August, Barnsley West Riding police authorities announced that John Gallagher, who was wanted on a coroner's warrant charged with the wilful murder of William Swann, glassblower, of Wombwell, on 6 June, had that morning been run to earth at Middlesbrough.

In Wombwell the first intimation to the local public of the news of Gallagher's arrest came when a telegram was posted in the window of Mr Lodge, newsagent. Wombwell police, however, knew of Gallagher's arrest a good hour before and Police Sergeant Playfoot was already on his way to Barnsley in anticipation of his proceeding to Middlesborough to take Gallagher in his charge from the Middlesbrough Police.

When Mrs Swann was told by police of Gallagher's arrest, she became very excited and talked in a rambling manner appeared to be very nervous. Mrs Swann kept a low profile for the remainder of the day and remained in a contemplative mood until police arrested her at midnight. She was conveyed to Barnsley by the 5.41am train. Gallagher, who had since his escape from Wombwell taken to the open road had arrived at his sister's house in Middlesborough in the company of another tramp, Gallagher being the worse for drink. Information soon reach the ears of the police and Gallagher's arrest was speedily effected. Gallagher was brought back to Barnsley in the company of Police Superintendent Quest and

John Gallagher, looking somewhat disheveled, seen here shortly after his capture in Middlesbrough.
Author's collection

Sergeant Playfoot. Since his departure from Wombwell via Sheffield, Gallagher had managed to find work by which he had survived, although he was very much worse for wear, having shaved very little and being severely weather-beaten. During his eight weeks on the road Gallagher had been in Manchester, Leeds, Bradford and finally, Harrogate, from where he had walked to Middlesbrough.

Great interest was expressed by the public when Gallagher made his first appearance at Barnsley West Riding Police Court on Wednesday morning. Even greater interest was shown when it was learned that Mrs Swann had also been arrested. Police presence in Westgate was strong to ensure public order was kept. When the public were allowed in to the building the courtroom was soon filled to capacity. The Bench comprised Messrs C Brady (Chairman), W Jackson, W A Durnford, M Gill, J T Field, W Washington and H Gamwell. Gallagher was described on the Court Sheet as John Gallagher, labourer, of no fixed abode, but who formerly resided in Milton Square, George Street, Wombwell. Gallagher was charged on a coroner's warrant with wilful murder etc. The name of Emily Swann also appeared on the list and the charge that appeared opposite her name was also that of wilful murder. Gallagher stepped smartly into the dock, Mrs Swann followed him in a shuffling manner. The proceedings were brief. Gallagher was wearing a shabby grey suit and had a scarf round his neck and watched the proceedings in a nervous manner. Those in the Court who knew him well could see that his time on the road had reduced his weight by a good two stones. Mrs Swann, dressed in black and wearing a hat, looked stern as she paid deep attention to the proceedings.

As soon as Gallagher and Swann were in the dock together, Superintendent Quest, said that he thought he would be able to prove that, on the night of 6 June last, a brutal murder was committed in Swann's house. Superintendent Quest went on to say:

The two prisoners were drinking together during the greater part of the afternoon, they afterwards went into the deceased's man's house and I think I shall be able to prove that the man Gallagher kicked Swann in such a manner that he died, and that Emil Swann encouraged him in so doing.

Towards the end of the proceedings, when Superintendent Quest, having requested that the prisoners be remanded until the following Wednesday, further asked that both prisoners be remanded to Wakefield, the whole Bench agreed without any hesitation. The prisoners were then removed from the courtroom. There was still a crowd outside the Court at two o'clock in the afternoon when a cab drew up outside in the customary fashion to take prisoners to Wakefield. To the dismay of the crowd the cab was not for Gallagher and Swan, who were eventually removed to the station by cab at 4.15pm. Both in Westgate and at the station the crowd remained, they were orderly but there was a hostile feeling. As the train had not arrived at the station Gallagher and Swann were kept out of reach of the crowd by placing them on the bridge (the same bridge that was taken down in recent years, and re-erected at Elsecar Heritage Centre). When the train drew up on the platform Gallagher and Swann were quickly placed in their carriage with a police escort and the blinds drawn to obscure them from view. As the train steamed out of the station and pulled slowly away from Barnsley, the crowd looked on with what the *Barnsley Independent* described as 'a severe countenance'.

Early on the following Wednesday the prisoners were brought from Wakefield to appear before Barnsley magistrates, where they were again remanded. During the brief proceedings, Mr Rideal rose and said:

In this case, your worships, I am instructed by the Treasury to prosecute the two prisoners on a charge of murder of the husband of the female prisoner. I am not ready at present to go on with the case, in which there are a large number of witnesses, some seventeen or eighteen …

Mr Rideal said he though it would be necessary for a special court should be held for the hearing. The prisoners were remanded to appear again at 10.00am the following Tuesday. A crowd of about a hundred waited outside the court and as the prisoners were taken to the station where they were placed in the waiting room with a strong police guard, curious onlookers packed the platforms. There was very little to see and once the train arrived Gallagher and Swann were speedily transferred to a carriage and the blinds were once again drawn.

On Tuesday 18 August, at the hearing before Barnsley West Riding Magistrates, Mr Rideal called seventeen witnesses for the prosecution. Before the first witness was called, the Chairman, Charles Brady, Esquire, asked the prisoners:

Does any one defend you at all? Have you a lawyer?

Gallagher, replying for both himself and Swann, simply said:

No, sir.

Mr Rideal then proceeded. One witness, a neighbour, living opposite the Swann's house, described how on 11 May between 8.30pm and 9.00pm, just as he had returned from work he saw William Swann come home. Gallagher was in the kitchen. Just as Swann entered the door, his wife struck him and knocked him down. On hearing this, Mrs Swann called out from the dock:

Oh, man alive.

The witness went on to say that a fight ensued between Swann and his wife, and Gallagher interfered. He first of all struck Swann with his fist and then began kicking him. During this attack on Swann, the witness heard Mrs Swann call out:

Kick the bastard to death. Kick the bloody swine. Kick him out of the way and I will help thee.

Then the witness said that on the Friday night before the murder he heard Swann and his wife quarrelling.

Another witness, Lavinia Ward, wife of Arthur Ward of 29 Alma Street, Wombwell, said, a week before the murder she heard Gallagher say he would kill Swann before he went away. Mrs Ward added that she had also heard Mrs Swann tell Gallagher to kill her husband on several occasions.

Police Sergeant Alfred John Minty, stationed at Wombwell, said on the night of William Swann's death he accompanied Sergeant Playfoot to the Swann's house. In the kitchen he found the body of the deceased lying on the floor with his head against the cupboard and a poker by his side. Mrs Swann and Mary Ann Ward were present but when he asked what had happened he could not get a satisfactory answer from either of them. Both women were very drunk. All Mrs Swann would say was:

He isn't dead is he? He can't be dead.

The prosecution's case against both prisoners was very strong. The prisoners had nothing to say in respect of the formal charge, and at the conclusion of the proceedings they were committed at Leeds Assizes, which were due to begin in October. As the two prisoners left the court Mrs Swann threw several kisses to her friends and relatives. Gallagher acknowledged no one. He didn't even turn his head to take a look around the courtroom. The prisoners were then taken to Wakefield in the usual way. There they would be given an ordinary diet and no work would be expected of them. They would also be allowed proper exercise during their detention.

On Monday 7 December John Gallagher and Emily Swann were brought into court at Leeds Town Hall at the Assizes to plead. Gallagher was placed in the dock and asked by Mr Justice Darling whether he was represented by counsel. When Gallagher answered in the negative, his Lordship, said to the Clerk that he understood the woman was represented and on being told that she was, his Lordship asked Gallagher if he would like to have counsel, to which Gallagher replied:

I should, please, my Lord.

His Lordship then told Gallagher:

I will see you are represented when the case is heard.

Gallagher and Swann's trial began on Wednesday 9 December. Mr E Tindall Atkinson, KC and Mr W J Waugh conducted the case for the prosecution. Gallagher was defended by Mr Mitchell Innes of Middle Temple, and Swann by Mr H Newell, of Bradford. The prisoners both stepped briskly into the dock. The Clerk announced:

The prisoners are charged that they on 6th June of the present year, at Wombwell, did feloniously, wilfully, by malice or forethought, did kill and murder William Swann.

Then intimating to Gallagher, the Clerk said:

Gallagher you have pleaded not guilty. Emily Swann, are you guilty of that charge or not!

Gallagher and Swann in the dock during their trial at Leeds Assizes. Author's collection

Then came the reply from Mrs Swann:

Not guilty, my Lord.

In his opening speech for the prosecution, Mr Tindall Atkinson said that the prisoners were charged jointly with the murder of William Swann and if the evidence was well founded there was not the slightest doubt that this man met his death under circumstances of the grossest brutality. The trial continued until Friday. Damning evidence against the couple was presented. The history of the many fights between husband and wife, Gallagher's involvement, the love affair that existed between Gallagher and Swann and the indiscreet utterances before numerous witnesses, where threats to kill William Swann had been made, seemed to leave little doubt that Gallagher and Swann had both conspired and intended to kill the man, whose murder for which they were both being now tried. Gallagher's defence was based on his infatuation for Mrs Swann. Besotted by love and inflamed by passion and drink, good sense overtook him but he did not intend to commit murder. Mrs Swann's defence was that although her actions were reprehensible and sinful, she intended nothing more than that her husband should receive a good thumping. The fact that Gallagher, shortly after his arrest had said that Mrs Swann had finished her husband off with the poker, seemed to have some credence, when one considers evidence proffered by several witnesses, that when he heard of William Swann's death, Gallagher had laughed and danced and said in joyful tones:

I haven't bloody well done it.

One wonders, if subconsciously he had convinced himself that the injuries inflicted on William Swann by himself had not caused the man's death, believing that his accomplice had in fact done the dirty deed. Gallagher's comments regarding Swann having finished her husband off with the poker was not revealed to the jury until after they had delivered their verdict. In any event, the evidence against the accused couple was so

Armley Gaol, Leeds, depicted in a nineteenth-century drawing. John D Murray collection

overwhelmingly strong, that it took them just half an hour to reach the verdict that both Gallagher and Swann were both guilty of wilful murder. Mr Justice Darling then passed sentence of death, but not before commenting that he had believed they had made the correct decision.

Before their execution both Gallagher and Swann listened to the ministrations of clergymen. In the condemned cell, Mrs Swann dictated letters to her eighty-year-old mother and to her sisters, requesting them to love her daughters Eleanor and little Elsie and to give little Raymond a kiss. John Gallagher and Emily Swann were executed together at Leeds on 29 December 1903. As they mounted the scaffold Gallagher appeared momentarily startled as Swann said to him:

Good morning, Johnny.

He replied:

Good morning love.

As Gallagher and Swann stood on the drop, executioner John Billington and his assistant quickly went about their business. Just as Billington pushed the lever, which withdrew the bolts and the drop fell, Mrs Swann uttered the words:

Goodbye, God bless you.

Then, Gallagher and Swann were despatched into eternity, as they plummeted to a quick and reportedly painless death. Later that morning, an inquest was held and afterwards the lovers, thirty-year-old John Gallagher and forty-two-year-old Emily Swann, suffered the indignity of being buried in quick lime lined graves, within Armley's precincts.

CHAPTER 12

The Barnsley Shooting Case
October 1903

He added that when he had been shot he did not see the shot fired but he had felt it.

Barnsley Borough Court was the scene of great interest on the morning of Thursday 5 November 1903, when the shooting case in Westgate, which had taken place the previous week, was heard before Dr Horne (deputy Mayor) and Mr W Jackson.

William Cooper, aged fifty-four, of 7 Surrey Yard, barman and former miner, stood in the dock, having been remanded from the previous Thursday. Cooper was charged with unlawfully and feloniously shooting and wounding Alice Maria Whittaker, George Thomas Whittaker and George Stanford, with intent to murder them at Barnsley on 28 October. Cooper was defended by Mr J Hewitt. He pleaded not guilty to the charges.

Fifteen-year-old Alice Maria Whittaker came to court directly from the Beckett Hospital from where she had been discharged earlier that morning following treatment of the injuries she had sustained during the shooting. She told the court that she resided with her grandmother, Mrs Moran, at the *Westgate Tavern*. She said she had known Cooper for about three years and he had been employed as a barman there for about two and-a-half years. She added that he had stopped working at the *Westgate Tavern* towards the end of September. On the 28 October, her grandmother sent her on an errand to buy bread, which necessitated her passing Cooper's house in Surrey Yard. She said she saw Cooper at his bedroom window. She continued about her business and, about five minutes later, passed through Surrey Yard on her return journey, where she stopped to talk for a few minutes to Mrs Longley, one of the yard's residents. Afterwards, as she proceeded up the yard in the direction of home, she was startled by hearing a shot fired. She looked down at her hands and saw that they were bleeding. She also felt a pain in her breast. She was carrying an umbrella in her right hand and two loaves in her left. These she dropped as she was shot. She screamed for help and her father came to her assistance. The court was shown the umbrella which was marked at the top with gunshots.

During cross-examination by Mr Hewitt, Miss Whittaker was asked:

> During the greater part of the time that you have known the prisoner he has been employed at the Westgate Tavern. Cooper was not living there as your grandmother's husband but more of a lodger. Has he been on great terms of intimacy with your grandmother and yourself? I mean to say as one of the family?

Alice Whittaker:	*Yes sir.*
Mr J Hewitt:	*Your grandmother is a widow?*
Alice Whittaker:	*Yes sir.*
Mr J Hewitt:	*And your father does not live with you at the tavern?*
Alice Whittaker	*No sir, but I live there.*
Mr J Hewitt:	*He [Cooper] has been a friend to you since September last?*
Alice Whittaker:	*Yes sir.*
Mr J Hewitt:	*I think he has been a kind sort of a friend. He has bought you flowers and brought some to the house?*
Alice Whittaker:	*Yes sir.*

During further questioning concerning Cooper's residency at the *Westgate Tavern*, Miss Whittaker said:

> Mr Cooper brought some colliery tools to the house but he had not, as far as I am aware, brought any furniture. He bought some pigeons and he reckoned the fowls were his ... I did not know he had won £10 on a shooting match or on a dog match. He did not buy me any presents except the flowers.

Mr J Hewitt: *He has always been kind to you?*

Alice Whittaker: *No he hasn't. He has always been trying to 'boss' over me.*

The courtroom found this comment by Miss Whittaker highly amusing and the proceedings were interrupted for a few moments during a long burst of laughter.

Mr J Hewitt: *Has the prisoner been cruel to you?*

Alice Whittaker: *He has been nasty sometimes.*

Mr J Hewitt: *Did he ever ill treat you?*

Alice Whittaker: *No sir.*

Mr J Hewitt: *A month before this* [the shooting incident] *he was told to leave, and he went into a house in Surrey Yard?*

Alice Whittaker: *Yes sir.*

Mr J Hewitt: *Did he ever threaten to do you any mischief?*

Alice Whittaker: *Yes; he threatened to shoot my grandmother and me.*

Mr J Hewitt: *When?*

Alice Whittaker: *The last week in September. It was a Friday about seven-thirty in the morning. The servant and myself were present. I was in the bar at the time. This was after Cooper had been told to leave. He came in and said 'Good Morning'. I didn't reply because I was unhappy with his behaviour the previous evening. On Thursday night some men were playing dominoes and one of them wanted some more beer, but Cooper would not serve him. My grandmother came and said the man should have some more beer if he wanted.*

Mr J Hewitt: *This was the origin of this quarrel which has been so much made of?*

Alice Whittaker: *Yes sir.*

Miss Whittaker continued to outline the lead up to shooting on 28 October. Following Cooper coming downstairs on Friday morning, after she had ignored him, Miss Whittaker told the court that he said:

'You get like your grandmother, and all the rest of them. I should like to shoot you both.' I was afraid he would carry out his threat. I had heard him make threatening remarks previously. My grandmother had fallen out with him before. On this previous night this seemed to have been just an ordinary quarrel and had nothing to do with me. On Wednesday 28 October I was walking down the centre of the yard, which is about twenty feet wide. When I was a few yards from Cooper's cottage I was walking near the wall and I could see him in his bedroom, sitting on the side of his bed.

Mr J Hewitt: *Are you sure it was possible to see him from where you were?*

Alice Whittaker: *I might have been mistaken. I'm sure it was him. I certainly wasn't frightened by what I saw and did not think that anything would afterwards happen.*

Following suggestions that Cooper had threatened to shoot the pigeons and fowls at the *Westgate Tavern* and that he had, in fact, being doing so when the shot rebounded from the wall opposite and accidentally wounded her, Miss Whittaker replied:

Cooper asked for his fowls and pigeons the last week in September, but they weren't given to him. I never heard him say anything about shooting the pigeons. There were some pigeons and fowls in the yard when I returned but I did not see any of them shot. Neither have I heard that any were shot.

Bench: *At the time you were shot are you of the opinion that the prisoner could clearly see you and was shooting directly at you?*

Alice Whittaker: *From where I was when I was shot I do not know if the prisoner could see me or if he was shooting directly at me. I know from that distance it would have been the simplest thing in the world to kill me. I am familiar with the cottage and the prisoner's bedroom, as I have*

> *visited that house many times since I was a child. I know if I had been in the bedroom in his place I could have seen the position I was first in when I came back into Surrey Yard.*

Miss Whittaker concluded her evidence by adding that she had complained to her grandmother about Cooper's threats.

George Thomas Whittaker, miner, of 37 New Street, Kinsley, near Hemsworth, son of Mrs Alice Moran and father of Alice Maria Whittaker, gave his evidence with a bandaged head. He said on 28 October he had arrived at the *Westgate Tavern* at about ten o'clock that morning to see his mother to discuss transferring the licence to himself. He saw his daughter, who was sitting knitting until his mother sent her on an errand. About ten minutes later he heard the report of gunfire coming from the direction of Surrey Yard, accompanied by cries of 'Murder!' He rushed out and saw his daughter. Her arms were covered with blood. He assisted her home, where she complained to him about Cooper's threat to shoot her. He went out to see if he could find Cooper. When he reached Cooper's cottage Sergeant Peacock was standing at the door. By this time George Stanford had also joined them. Mr Whittaker said he then heard another report and immediately fell to the ground having been shot in the back, on the back of the head, and behind the left ear. He suffered considerable loss of blood from the wounds and was assisted into the *Westgate Tavern* before being conveyed to the Beckett Hospital for treatment. He was still under the care of Dr Hanan. Mr Whittaker produced the waistcoat he had been wearing. It was perforated with shot. He added that he had been obliged to speak to Cooper previously about his conduct and that it had been necessary to complain to police because Cooper had disobeyed his orders, but not during the last twelve months. During cross-examination by Mr Hewitt, Mr Whittaker said, when he came to the *Westgate Tavern* he assumed the management. Regarding the prisoner's conduct towards his mother, Mr Whittaker said that he did not know that Cooper had been kind to her, but did know that he had been unkind when he 'bumped her lug' and caused a wound on her head. However, he had not seen Cooper assault his mother. He added that when he had been shot he did not see the shot fired but he had felt it. He said he did not notice the fowls and pigeons in the yard. He was concerned about his daughter and himself. He could not suggest why Cooper should shoot at him.

George Stanford, labourer, of 30 Osborne Street, said that on the morning in question he was at his sister's house in Roper Street, when he heard a shot fired and ran to see what happened. When he arrived in Surrey Yard, he heard a second shot and saw Mr Whittaker fall to the ground. He also felt the shot penetrate his left arm and left breast When cross-examined by Mr Hewitt, Mr Stanford said he had no quarrel with Cooper, as he was a complete stranger to him and he could provide no reason why Cooper should shoot at him. Mr Stanford added that in his opinion the shots were direct and had not rebounded from the wall opposite.

Alice Maria Moran, widow and licensee of the *Westgate Tavern*, said that her granddaughter had lived with her from being a month old. She said she had known Cooper for about two-and-half years. Cooper was engaged as barman and she paid him £1 a week and also paid 3s a week rent for the cottage in which he lived. Mrs Moran said she had discharged Cooper, on 24 September, since when he had been a source of annoyance to her. He had come to the house and threatened to blow her brains out. On one occasion he came to the window with a knife and said he would cut her liver out. He also said he would ruin her and the *Westgate Tavern*. On Friday week Cooper came into her bedroom and threatened to knock her through the wall. He asked for money, said he was 'stoney broke' and had pawned his clothes. She would not give him any money but said she told him to go where he had spent it. She went on to say that on the morning of the shooting ten minutes after her granddaughter had gone out, she was in the kitchen when she heard a shot, then Alice cry out, 'Cooper has shot me!' Cross-examined by Mr Hewitt, Mrs Moran denied that Cooper had been living with her as her husband. She was under notice at her public house. She said that the prisoner was formerly a miner but had never given her his earnings nor

£10 he had received as a result of a wager. She said she had never heard Cooper say he would shoot the pigeons if she did not let him have them. The fowls belonged to her but the pigeons were Cooper's.

The next witness, Clara Longley, of 10 Surrey Yard, said only that she had heard shots fired and saw the girl injured. Sergeant Peacock said that on the morning of the shooting he was in the vicinity of Surrey Yard when he heard shots being fired and saw Alice Whittaker bleeding from the arms. He went to the cottage occupied by Cooper and found the door locked. He shouted to Cooper to open the door but got no response. He then looked up at the bedroom window and saw Cooper who shouted out, 'Look out, stand back, or I'll shoot some more of you!' Sergeant Peacock said he then saw Cooper put the gun to his shoulder and fire, and Whittaker and Stanford were injured. The sergeant then called upon Cooper to open the door, and he replied, 'All right, I'll come quietly.' With that Cooper came downstairs and unlocked the door. Sergeant Peacock asked Cooper to put the gun down. Cooper then threw the gun to the ground and as he did so exclaimed, 'Stand away, it's loaded, and may go off.' Cooper was then apprehended. When he was told he would be detained at the Police Station Cooper replied, 'I was shooting at some pigeons, and I hit her.' Cooper was searched and some gun caps were found on him. Sergeant Peacock said when he searched Cooper's house he found twenty-three gun caps, four wads, a flask containing powder, another flask containing shot and a ram-rod. When charged, Cooper said, 'What have I to murder her for? I have never had anything against her' in respect of the girl's father, he said, 'I have nothing against him in the least, only against the old woman,' and as for Mr Stanford, he said, 'I don't know the man. It was the pigeons I wanted to shoot.'

Inspector Harris corroborated part of Sergeant Peacock's evidence and commented on removing the injured from the *Westgate Tavern* to the Beckett Hospital. He said the weapon used was a muzzle-loader, and on the nipple was found an undischarged cap. In the flasks were 1oz of powder and 1½ oz of shot.

Dr Hanan, house surgeon at the Beckett Hospital, gave evidence concerning the three injured, whom he had treated. Alice Whittaker had gunshot wounds on her hands, on the top of her arms and chest. Her injuries were such that it was necessary to detain her in hospital. George Whittaker had sustained the most serious injuries of the three victims. Some shot had to be removed from the back of his scalp. Some shot was also extracted from George Stanford's scalp. Dr Hanan said all the wounds inflicted were of a superficial nature, the shot having just penetrated the skin and come out again. In his opinion, the person who fired the gun must have hit all three victims from a side-long position.

In Cooper's defence Mr Hewitt submitted that a *prima facia* case had not been made out. He said there had been no previous quarrel between Cooper and the persons injured, and he could have no motive for shooting them. Mr Hewitt went on to say:

> *In the case of the girl, the many kindnesses he had shown were inconsistent with that supposition. Why did he shoot them? The explanation was simple enough. He and Mrs Moran had lived together as husband and wife, but a difference had arisen. Cooper had some pigeons, which were kept on Mrs Moran's premises, and when he asked for them, she refused to give them to him. He then said he would shoot them and was perfectly within his rights in so doing, there was no unlawful act about that. The shooting of these people was a mere accident, as the evidence of the prosecution itself went to affirm. The persons injured had no feeling against the prisoner, nor he against them, and the superficial nature of the wounds disproved any deliberate shooting at them.*

Mr Hewitt said the charge was frivolous and asked that his client be set free. The Bench did not agree with Cooper's defence deciding the case should be heard by a higher tribunal and committed him to stand trial at the Leeds Assizes to be held early in December.

On Saturday 6 December William Cooper came up before Mr Justice Darling. He was indicted for the attempted murder of Alice Martha Whittaker, George Thomas Whittaker and

William Cooper. Author's collection

George Stanford by shooting at them with a gun at Barnsley on 28 October. Mr Sanderson appeared for the prosecution and Mr Middleton defended. At the commencement of the trial Mr Middleton said that his client wished to withdraw his previous plea of not guilty, and plead guilty to shooting with intent to do bodily harm to the two men. Mr Middleton said his client maintained that he did not shoot at the girl. He said the prosecution had agreed to accept the plea and would not proceed with the case concerning Miss Whittaker. His Lordship agreed to this request and the charge of attempting to murder Alice Maria Whittaker was not proceeded with.

Mr Sanderson outlined the case. He said that for some time the prisoner was employed as barman at the *Westgate Tavern* and lived close by. He had been discharged by Mrs Moran, the landlady and after that he seemed to have harboured a good deal of revenge. Mr Sanderson went on to describe the events of 28 October and concluded by saying that when the prisoner was charged with murder he had commented, 'I have nothing to murder her for. I have nothing against any of them, except the old woman.'

The defence was that the shooting was accidental, the prisoner being engaged shooting at pigeons at the time. Mr Sanderson then pointed out that nobody had seen any pigeons lying about and the prisoner had pleaded guilty to shooting with intent. Cooper said that the pigeons and the fowls were his. He alleged that Mrs Moran would not let him have them and he had told her on 27 October that if she did not he would shoot them. Cooper then said that when he fired the first shot he hit one of them and it disappeared inside a hole. He said he had told the police sergeant about this but he did not inspect the place for two days, and it was 'worried with rats', as many as nine 'fowls' disappeared in one night.

Mr Middleton turned to the medical evidence, which he said showed that the wounds were only of a superficial character and not at all dangerous. He concluded by saying that very little harm had been done, and asked that under these circumstances, he hoped his Lordship would exercise such leniency, as he felt to be consistent with the case.

Mr Justice Darling said he thought the prosecution had made the right decision in accepting the prisoner's plea. Before he gave a sentence of five years' penal servitude to Cooper, his Lordship commented, 'He [Cooper] shot at a distance which would not kill these people, but, if he did not shoot with intent to murder them, he did so meaning to do them grievous bodily harm.'

CHAPTER 13

Murder of a Farm Bailiff, Dodworth 1948

Without being flippant, I ask, how could a man experienced in shooting have made such a hopelessly bad shot?

Barnsley West Riding Magistrates' Court was at the centre of attention, for members of the public throughout the area, on Tuesday 2 March 1948, as news had already reached their ears of a brutal murder that had taken place at Dodworth the previous day. Sixty-six-year-old, farmer Frank Kilburn, of Field Head Farm, Silkstone, was charged with the murder of farm bailiff, sixty-five-year-old, John William Barlow of Croft Top Farm, off High Street, Dodworth. Frank Kilburn, looking haggard and drawn and was without collar and tie, as he walked slowly to the dock escorted by police officers. He gripped the dock rail as he listened to the brief proceedings.

Police Superintendent Dunn, said:

Kilburn is alleged to have murdered Barlow by shooting him with a gun, at Croft Top Farm. At about 8.50am on Monday information was received at the police office at Dodworth that Barlow had been shot in the face with a shotgun. The man died in Beckett Hospital at 12.40pm the same day ...

Following the shooting on Monday morning, the police had commenced their inquiries at 9.00am. That evening, their inquiries had led them to the home of Frank Kilburn. Kilburn was visited there by Police Inspector Smith and Police Constable Myers, from where he was taken to Dodworth Police Station and afterwards to Barnsley West Riding Police headquarters for enquiries. At the police headquarters when he was cautioned and charged by Police Constable Barnish, Kilburn replied:

The dog was just at the back of him. He was bending down pouring some milk in the pail. I shot at the dog and hit him. Now I have told you all I have got to say.

Superintendent Dunn asked the magistrates for a remand and also requested a report as to Kilburn's mental condition.

Acting for Kilburn, Mr W Winter said:

I would like to invoke the clemency of the Superintendent to permit Kilburn to see his son.

A request to which the magistrates' clerk, Mr P St John Carrington, was prompted to remark:

I am sure you will receive every facility and assistance from the police.

The inquest on John William Barlow was opened at Barnsley Town Hall, on Wednesday 3 March, by Coroner C J Haworth, Esquire. Evidence of identification was given by the dead man's daughter, Mrs Edna Parkinson, wife of bricklayer, Edward Parkinson, of Junction Street, Barnsley.

Medical evidence was given by the doctor who had attended to the injured farm bailiff when he arrived at the hospital and by the pathologist who had conducted the post-mortem examination.

Dr J W L Haddon, resident surgical officer at Beckett Hospital, said that Barlow was admitted about 9.10am, suffering from gun shot wounds on the side of his face. He died at 12.40pm the same day.

Professor P L Sutherland, Home Office Pathologist, said:

I carried out a post-mortem examination and the cause of death was haemorrhage and shock from gun shot wounds on the right side of the face. The wounds were caused by pellets.

The coroner then addressed the jury, saying:

> *I have received notice from the Clerk to the Barnsley West Riding Justice that a man named Kilburn has been charged with the murder of Barlow and in those circumstances it will not be necessary to proceed any further today…*

The inquest was adjourned to a later date.

Committal proceedings took place at Barnsley West Riding Magistrates' Court on Tuesday 6 April.

Outlining the case for the Director of Public Prosecutions, Mr W Lewis said:

> *I think I can quite properly put the facts very shortly because as I see it, they are not in dispute. Kilburn was a farmer, he had actually been a farm bailiff and probably spent most of his life in the farming world. He and Barlow had known each other for a number of years. While it is not part of my duty to show that Kilburn had any motive for inflicting injury on Barlow it might be of assistance if I mention that towards the end of January or possibly in the middle of February Barlow had introduced Kilburn to two other farmers, two younger men called Batley. The immediate reason for the introduction was that Kilburn had some heifers, and he felt he had not sufficient fodder to justify keeping them. The Batley brothers bought these heifers from him. Hardly had Kilburn sold them at a reasonable price than he regretted his action and wanted the heifers back. My own view is it does not provide any motive, but it might be Kilburn brooded over the sale of the heifers and, as Barlow had effected the introduction which brought about the sale felt some grievance against Barlow, ill-founded and misguided though such a grievance might be…*

Mr Lewis went on to say that on Monday 1 March Kilburn got up early, which was his usual custom. He set about his usual duties at the farm, then broke off about 7.30pm and changed into clothes in which he usually went to market. As he was leaving the farm his son asked him where he was going. Kilburn replied that he was taking the day off. A little after 8.00am Kilburn was in the vicinity of Croft Top Farm.

He was seen making his way towards the cowshed by the farm's owner, Mrs Barratt. At about 8.30am Mrs Barratt was in the kitchen when she heard a noise outside the door. On opening the door she was confronted by the horrific sight of her employee, farm bailiff John Barlow, covered with blood and with serious injuries to the face and jaw. Mr Lewis then went on to give details of the injured man's admission to the Beckett Hospital and mentioned that when police officers saw Mr Barlow at the hospital they ascertained that he was fully aware of the fact that he might die at any moment. Although Mr Barlow was unable to speak he was able to write down the answers to the questions which were put to him. The answers to these questions effectively became John Barlow's dying declaration:

> *I make this statement being in immediate fear of death. I understand what you are saying to me although I cannot speak but I will nod or shake my head in answer to your questions.*

When asked to write down the name of the person who had shot him, Barlow wrote 'Kilburn'. When asked what he had been shot with, he wrote 'Gun'. The law was quite clear in a case of this kind regarding the fact that the accused person was not present when a dying declaration was made by a victim of murder. As a result of this deathbed interview the police went and arrested Kilburn.

There was a .410 shot gun missing from Kilburn's home on the day of the shooting. Frank Kilburn did not arrive home until the late evening. His son and daughter-in-law were curious to know where he had been. He simply replied he had been somewhere he hadn't been for many a year. When they questioned him further on the subject they were told:

> *I don't ask you where you go when you go out. I am not telling you where I have been.*

He had the shotgun with him. Police were already at the farm when he returned home. Police Inspector Smith and Police Constable Myers, on discovering that Frank Kilburn was not at home, kept observation on Field Head Farm and at 9.50pm saw Kilburn in an outbuilding. Inspector Smith said:

I shone my light on him and as I approached he shouted 'Hullo.'
I replied, 'Hullo, Dad.' I saw the barrel of a gun behind his back.
He was in the act of closing the door when I grabbed the gun and
handed it to PC Myers. I then seized Kilburn and took him into
the house. The gun was cocked and the constable extracted a live
cartridge from the breech. In Kilburn's pocket we found six live
cartridges.

When charged with murder, Kilburn had commented that he had been shooting at the dog. Concerning that statement, Mr Lewis for the prosecution, said:

I feel I must analyse that statement. You will hear from witnesses
that Kilburn is a man who has always been used to handling
guns and by implication, being a farmer of many years'
experience, it will be appreciated he has always been used to
dealing with dogs.

The defendant's son, farm labourer John Bruce Kilburn, when questioned about his father's shooting ability, said his father was a medium shot. During questioning, he said his father was diabetic and had been taking insulin twice a day. John Kilburn added that his mother's death between three and four years previously had depressed his father considerably. He had complained about his head recently and had slept very badly.

John Barlow had a dog which was his constant companion and which habitually laid outside the cowshed whenever he was at work inside. The dog was quiet and docile in every way. With regard to Kilburn's statement that he had been shooting at the dog, when he accidentally hit Barlow, experiments conducted at the forensic science laboratory, to ascertain the maximum height at which the jaw of a man the same height as Barlow would be when pouring milk into a can from a bucket and in relation to the shoulder of a man firing a shot gun. A straight trajectory would be at least three feet high and the dog was nothing approaching that height. Lewis Charles Nickolls, director of the North Eastern Forensic Science Laboratory at Wakefield confirmed these findings. Regarding this, Mr Lewis said:

Without being flippant, I ask how could a man experienced in shooting have made such a hopelessly bad shot? How did Kilburn know when he left home that something was going to arise in which he would require a gun? Why did he take the gun with him and why was the gun loaded when he got to the cowshed?

Mr Lewis suggested that taken as a whole, the circumstances discounted any question that the shooting of Barlow was accidental.

Dr J W L Haddon said that when he was admitted to Beckett Hospital, Barlow was suffering from shock and had severe difficulty in breathing, owing to severe gun shot wounds to the right side of the face and jaw, which was shattered. In reply to a question put to him by Mr P Stanley Price, for the defence, Dr Haddon said:

From the position of the wounds I would say that the man who shot Barlow had been standing at the side of him and it did not look as though Barlow had been looking at the man who fired.

Professor P L Sutherland, the Home Office pathologist who conducted the post-mortem examination said he counted thirty-three separate openings on the right side of the face.

With regard to what was generally presumed to have been the motive for the shooting. farmer Eric Batley, of Whitley Bridge, Goole, told the court that early in the year, in January, he was in company with Kilburn and Barlow to Dodworth, and after leaving Barlow, he went with Kilburn to his farm and purchased ten heifers at £20 each from him. However, on the following Friday, Mr Batley said that Kilburn wanted him to let him have the heifers back, and offered him an additional £1 for each beast to cover a weeks' fodder and carriage. However, Mr Batley said he had told Kilburn:

It was poor business and a bargain was a bargain.

About a fortnight before the shooting, Mr Batley said he saw Kilburn and Barlow together in Doncaster pig market, when they appeared to be on good terms with each other.

At the end of the proceedings Kilburn was committed to take his trial at the next Leeds Assizes.

Frank Kilburn was tried before Mr Justice Streatfield on Tuesday 4 May. Mr H B H Hylton-Foster-KC, prosecuted. Kilburn was defended by Mr G Raymond Hinchcliffe, KC, and he pleaded not guilty.

G R Hinchcliffe, KC: *What made you shoot at the dog?*

Kilburn: *I thought it was going for me. It was snarling and showing its teeth … When I realised John Barlow had taken the full force of the shot I saw him get up and start to walk out. He said, 'Look what you've done.' I was going to look but Barlow walked off to his house. That made me think he was not badly hurt. I saw blood on his face and it upset my nerves afterwards. I did nothing for a while only stand still. It put me off my balance altogether. I did not accompany Barlow to his cottage because I felt too upset and nervous.*

G R Hinchcliffe, KC: *It is suggested that you very much resented the sale of the ten heifers to the Batleys and because of the resentment you shot and murdered Barlow?*

Kilburn: *Nothing of the kind. I had no ill feeling at all against him. I had no grievance against him whatever because we had always been the best of friends … I reloaded the gun because I thought about shooting myself if I saw the police coming …*

At the conclusion of the witness evidence, which was much the same as that given in the committal proceedings at Barnsley, the jury retired to consider their verdict. They returned an hour and three-quarters later with a guilty verdict but with a strong recommendation to mercy.

In addressing the prisoner in the dock, Mr Justice Streatfield told Kilburn:

> *... the recommendation of the jury will be forwarded by me to the proper quarter. In the meantime it is my duty to pass upon you the sentence prescribed by law, which is that unless His Majesty shall otherwise order, you shall suffer death by hanging.*

On Friday 11 June, *The Times* reported that the Home Secretary had seen fit to request that His Majesty should grant Frank Kilburn a reprieve, having considered the jury's recommendation to mercy.

CHAPTER 14

Killing of an Unfaithful Wife at the Milton Arms Hotel, Hemingfield 1952

While one does not wish to speak disrespectfully of the dead, in this case, it must be apparent that Mrs Caddick was an utterly worthless woman.

On the evening of Tuesday 18 November 1952, forty-six-year-old miner Alfred Caddick and his forty-year-old wife of twenty-two years, Edith, of Foley Avenue, Wombwell, were drinking in the taproom of the *Milton Arms Hotel*, in Cemetery Road, Hemingfield, with William and Elsie Clarke, who lived nearby, at 20 Quest Avenue, with whom Mrs Caddick had recently been lodging, having been estranged from her husband and children for about ten weeks. Edith Caddick was well known among the

The Milton Arms Hotel, *Hemingfield.* Chris and Pearl Sharp of Old Barnsley

regulars at the *Milton Arms Hotel*, not only as a long standing customer, but more recently, as a part-time barmaid. At a little before ten o'clock Mrs Caddick made enquiries at the bar regarding the time, saying that she wanted to catch the 10.10pm bus to Wombwell, then left the hotel alone, leaving her husband behind drinking with the Clarkes. At 10.18pm Alfred Caddick finished his drink and was also seen to leave the premises. Soon afterwards, Ethel Caddick was fatally injured at the hotel's entrance. She had been stabbed in the back. She died at the scene and Arthur Caddick was taken into police custody.

On Wednesday 19 November Alfred Caddick was brought before the Bench in custody. Superintendent Dunn asked for a remand to prison for one week in order that investigations could be completed and the facts placed before the Director of Public Prosecutions. The Clerk of the Court, Mr P St John Carrington told Caddick that he strongly advised him to have a solicitor and to apply for Legal Aid, to which the prisoner appeared somewhat perplexed when he replied:

I don't know.

The Bench took a decision to grant Caddick free Legal Aid and appointed Mr A S McKenzie to act for him. They also granted the prisoner a certificate for counsel. Throughout the entire hearing, which lasted only seven minutes, Caddick was severely distressed and in an apparent state of collapse, resulting in it being necessary for two policemen to assist him in the dock. Following these brief proceedings the prisoner was half carried from the Court, all the while weeping and shaking his head.

An inquest was opened and adjourned before Coroner S H B Gill, Esquire, at Hoyland Town Hall on Friday 21 November. Police Sergeant A W Butroid, of the West Riding Police, stationed at Hoyland, said he was called to the *Milton Arms Hotel* at Hemingfield on Wednesday evening, where upon arrival he found Mrs Caddick on the floor in the porchway. She was being attended to by Dr Dickenson, of Wombwell but the woman died at the scene in his (Sergeant Butroid's)

Hoyland Town Hall, where the inquest was held. Author's collection.

presence. Sergeant Butroid went on to say that, following the woman's death, he had the body removed to Hoyland mortuary, where Dr David E Price performed a post-mortem examination.

Chief Inspector W Bell said it was not intended to offer any further evidence for the time being and requested the coroner to adjourn the inquest for at least six weeks. In reply the Coroner said he would adjourn the inquest until 8 January 1953.

Edith Caddick's funeral took place during the afternoon Saturday 22 September. A small crowd of around a hundred people, most of them women, some of them pushing perambulators and virtually all of them wearing head squares and shawls, waited outside the gates of Wombwell Cemetery for the cortege to arrive. After the cortege had passed through the gates part of the crowd surged forward, clearly with the intention of following the mourners to the graveside. They were prevented from doing so by the police who barred their way into the cemetery and locked the iron gates shut behind the mourners. The small band of mourners were led to the graveside by the Rev A Cockayne, of St George's Church, Jump. A bunch of white chrysanthemums, bearing a card with the message 'To my dearest wife, from Alf', was amongst the floral tributes. There was a wreath from the deceased woman's children, one from her mother and sisters and another from her neighbours and friends.

On Monday 12 January 1953, miner and amateur conjurer, Alfred Caddick appeared before Barnsley West Riding Magistrates charged with the wilful murder of his wife, allegedly by stabbing her in the heart with a toy dagger belonging to their twelve-year-old son. Caddick pleaded not guilty and reserved his defence.

Representing the Director of Public Prosecutions, Mr J M Evelyn, outlined the case. Mr Evelyn said that the Caddicks, who had been married for twenty-two years, had not been happy together for some time. The couple had frequently argued and after hearing the evidence the Bench might think that the motive for murder was clearly jealousy. At the latter end of September Mrs Caddick left home and was estranged from her husband for the remaining eight weeks of her life. She went to live with Mr and Mrs Clarke at Hemingfield. Mrs Caddick worked for an engineering firm but later took a job at the *Milton Arm Hotel*. During the two weeks before her death she had been associating with Thomas Melling of Hemingfield and her husband was aware of that association. On Saturday 15 November Mrs Caddick returned home again. On the evening of Tuesday 18 November both the accused and Mrs Caddick went to Hemingfield to collect some clothes she had left at the Clarkes. The accused went to the *Milton Arms Hotel* while his wife went to the Clarkes' house in Quest Avenue. Later in the evening Mrs Caddick joined her husband at the *Milton Arms Hotel,* accompanied by Mr and Mrs Clarke. They all drank together and everything seemed perfectly friendly. Mrs Caddick left her husband drinking with the Clarkes, saying she was going to catch a bus. Her husband was to follow on later. While Mrs Caddick was standing at the bus stop, Thomas Melling passed by and she called him over. Not long afterwards the accused came out of the hotel and saw his wife with Melling. He crossed over the road to the bus stop and caught hold of his wife's shoulders and using a profanity said to her she was not coming to his xxxx house tonight. The accused then allegedly thrust at Melling's groin, injuring him. Melling went over to the hotel for assistance and the accused followed him. Moments later the accused came out of the hotel accompanied by Mr Clarke just as Mrs Caddick was crossing the road towards them. The accused ran to meet her, then stabbed her. Mrs Clarke also suffered a slight head injury caused by the accused. Mrs Caddick was carried into the doorway of the hotel and her husband appeared to be extremely distressed.

Included among the many exhibits on display in the courtroom were bloodstained clothing worn by the deceased woman, a sharp pointed toy dagger, leather sheath, a pair of scissors, the accused's overcoat, white silk scarf and trousers, conjuring trick apparatus, which Caddick had in his possession when arrested, and several photographs taken by a police officer on the night of the crime scene.

The first witness was Dr J M Dickenson, of Hough Lane, Wombwell, who said he was called to the *Milton Arms Hotel*, where he found Mrs Caddick lying in the vestibule. She was dead. The accused was leaning over the body and saying:

Wake up Edie

or some such words. Dr Dickenson said he also examined Melling, who had sustained a stab wound in his groin.

Defending, Mr J E Parris, in his cross-examination of the witness, asked Dr Dickenson with regard to the accused:

Would it be too high to say he was out of his mind?

Dr Dickenson replied:

I think that would be going too far.

The accused man's thirteen-year-old son, Douglas, was the next witness called. From the court exhibits, Douglas was shown a dagger and a sheath, which he identified as his own property. He said he found the dagger in Wombwell Woods and everyone at home knew he had it. It was normally kept behind a knife box in the kitchen and he had last seen the dagger a month before his mother's death. Continuing with his evidence, Douglas said his mother left home in September and came back the second week in November. When his father asked him if he wanted his mother to come back he had replied in the affirmative and when she did come back, they appeared to get on all right. With regard to the relationship between Douglas's parents, Mr Parriss asked:

Your father loved your mother very much indeed?

Douglas Caddick: *Yes sir.*
J E Parriss: *He was heartbroken when she went away with this man Melling?*
Douglas Caddick: *Yes sir.*
J E Parriss: *And he was overjoyed when she came back.*
Douglas Caddick: *Yes sir.*

When Arthur Caddick was taken into custody, some apparatus with which he performed conjuring tricks was found on his person. One particular trick involved the use of a knife, which seemed to explain why Caddick had a knife on him the night he stabbed his wife. Douglas said that his father was a very good conjuror. He knew of a trick that was done with a knife and three pieces of paper although he had never seemed the trick performed.

Spencer R Hazzard, landlord of the *Milton Arms Hotel* Hemingfield, said on the night of Edith Caddick's death he saw her with the accused and Mr and Mrs Clarke drinking in the tap room and they all looked quite normal. At 10.25pm Mr Clarke showed him a knuckle injury and he saw Mr Melling, who had blood on him. When Mr Hazzard went out to the hotel vestibule, he saw Mrs Caddick lying on the floor with the accused trying to hold her and asking her to speak. Mr Hazzard said he fetched an overcoat and put it under Mrs Caddick's head. On being cross-examined by Mr Parris, Mr Hazzard said that the accused appeared 'desperately perturbed'.

Thomas Melling, a thirty-four-year-old single miner, said he had known Edith Caddick for three or four months. They had been intimate with each other. He was aware that she had been living away from her husband. He had spent Tuesday evening in Hemingfield WMC, leaving there about 10.10pm. He was making his way to the *Milton Arms Hotel,* when he heard a shout. He saw Mrs Caddick across the road and went over to talk to her. Melling went on:

> *I wasn't there a minute when the accused came like a madman and started to shake his wife's shoulders. He told her 'You are not coming to stay to my house tonight!' Then I caught it, he stabbed me, his hand came up from behind his coat and he stabbed me in the left hip. I saw nothing in his hand. I felt as sick as a dog…*

Melling said he went across to the hotel to ask for assistance and while he was there the accused came in and asked for an ambulance. Melling said:

> *Nobody spoke to him and he went out and slammed the door.*

The pathologist, Dr Price, then gave the medical evidence, followed by Fred Bell of 1 Fitzwilliam Street, Hemingfield, who said he was walking towards the hotel at about 10.17pm, when he heard a man shout. He saw Melling with the accused and Mrs Caddick. During the course of his evidence, Mr Bell said:

> *Mr Clarke went back into the public house and Caddick went towards his wife and put his arms around her. She was now standing inside the front doorway of the hotel but she slid down the side of the wall on to the step. Caddick ran into the hotel. Mrs Caddick managed to sit up, she shook herself and staggered over to the other side of the doorway. Again she collapsed on to the floor. Caddick rushed out again shouting 'Edie, Edie, where are you?' I went over to help to pick her up.*

During his evidence, William Clarke said he had gone outside the hotel at the request of the accused. He heard Mrs Caddick call him then:

I turned and Caddick stood up against me. I got a sharp dig in the wrist. When I drew away I asked him what was wrong with him and he did not answer. He was holding a sharp pointed instrument. Caddick then ran round me towards his wife and then I heard him say 'Oh! What have I done.' Mrs Caddick slumped forward onto him. I went back into the hotel. I came out again and saw the accused with his wife in the hotel doorway. Mrs Caddick had her head on her husband's knee. Caddick said to me, 'Bill, can't you find us somewhere different from this.'

During cross-examination Mr Clarke said that as long as he had known the accused, since their schooldays, he had always regarded him as a quiet inoffensive little man and as a good living decent chap.

Herbert Hyde, of 15 Quest Avenue, said, on seeing Caddick rush up to his wife, he heard him say:

I have done it. Edith I did not mean to do it. I love you.

Caddick then shouted for a doctor and then went into the hotel, coming out again almost immediately. Mr Hyde went into the hotel and Caddiuck came rushing in again asking for a doctor. On seeing Melling lying on a sette, Caddick said:

I don't mean for you.

Police Constable Leonard Howden, stationed at Jump, said, as a result of a message, he went to Hemingfield and arrived at the *Milton Arms Hotel* at 10.34pm and found Mrs Caddick lying on the vestibule floor. He saw the accused coming out of the hotel yard and challenged him but Caddick took no notice and walked straight past into the hotel main entrance, where he crouched down beside his wife and said:

I didn't mean to do it Edie. Edie don't leave me.

PC Howden said he cautioned Caddick but again received no reply:

I asked him what he had stabbed her with and he put his hand into the pocket of his overcoat. I place my hand into the pocket and took out a pair of scissors ... I was later placed in charge of the accused during a subsequent investigation. He appeared very distressed and said 'Let me go to Edith, is she alright? Oh my God what have I done. Why didn't she go straight home.' When the accused was later questioned he said, 'I am not saying anything, let me go to her.' He was continually walking up and down, holding his head in his hands, then banging his head against the wall, kneeling down and praying and picking loose threads out of the carpet on the floor. He was continually talking and said, 'I didn't mean to do it. Why did I do it? You should have gone home. Why did I come here tonight. I did not do it with those scissors which you took from me. It was a dagger. I threw it into a field. It was a toy dagger but I fixed it up. I saw them at the bus stop and he said "You can't have her back." I had a knife in my pocket and I told her to go home but she stood at the bus stop with him. He is only a bit of a lad but that is enough ..." The accused also had three pen knives in his pocket as well as the scissors and he explained that he used them for conjuring tricks ...'

Police Constable Alan Hill, stationed at Wombwell, said he had found a leather knife sheath on the edge of a roof of a building at the rear of the hotel and a dagger sticking in the ground nearby.

Caddick made an application for a defence certificate, which was granted. At the close of the hearing, chairman of the Bench, T H Burrows, Esquire, complimented the prosecution on the very fair way in which they had presented the case. Caddick was then committed to take his trial at Leeds Assizes, commencing in February 1953.

Alfred Caddick's trial at Leeds Assizes before Mr Justice Havers began on Thursday 19 March 1953 and lasted for three days. Mr H B Hylton-Foster, QC, assisted by Mr C Aarvold , conducted the case for the prosecution. The prisoner was defended by Mr E J Parris, assisted by Mr R C Hutchinson. During the trial Caddick wore a dark suit with a white shirt and black tie.

Mr Hylton-Foster outlined the case for the prosecution. He said the Caddick family consisted of the accused man, his wife, a married daughter, eighteen-year-old, Alfred and the youngest child, Douglas, aged thirteen. As long as the older boy could remember there had been fights between Caddick and his wife. Over the past ten years Caddick's wife had left home and returned several times. About August last year she was known to be associating with a man named Melling. In September the wife went to live at Hemingfield with the Clarke family. She got work at Chapeltown and used to meet Melling to commit adultery with him. After leaving the Clarke household she went to the *Milton Arms Hotel* where she lived for four days. On 15 November, she returned to Caddick. The accused man was glad to have her back and all seemed well. Mr Hylton Foster then went on to outline the events of Tuesday 18 November. Much of the witness evidence followed that heard at the committal proceedings before Barnsley magistrates. As the trial progressed the defence called a surprise witness. Once the trial was underway the medical evidence was heard. West Riding Pathologist Dr David E Price, of Wakefield, described Edith Caddick's injuries:

> *There was an incised wound just over half an inch long penetrating between the eighth and ninth ribs, travelling inward, upward and straight forward into the apex of the heart. Death was as a result of shock and haemorrhage.*

When Thomas Melling, who gave his address as 122 Cemetery Road, Hemingfield, was placed on the witness stand, he was asked what were the relations between himself and Mrs Caddick during the four months that he knew her, he replied:

> *Friendship, sir.*

During further questioning, Melling admitted to being intimate with Mrs Caddick. Cross-examining Melling, Mr Parris asked:

Are you not thoroughly ashamed of the part you have played in the tragedy?

Melling: *No. I am not.*
Mr E J Parris: *Is it not clear to you but for your adultery with this woman she would be alive today?*

To this question Melling gave no reply.

Mr E J Parris: *You are not ashamed.*
Melling: *I said I wasn't.*
Mr E J Parris: *When you met Mrs Caddick you knew she was married?*
Melling: *Yes.*
Mr E J Parris: *Did you commit adultery with her the first time you met?*
Melling: *No. It was three weeks later.*

During further questioning, it was revealed that Melling would meet Mrs Caddick at the *Milton Arms Hotel* and they used to go for walks in the fields and woods. In reply to Mr Parris Melling said when he walked Mrs Caddick home to Quest Avenue they had intercourse on the way.

Mr E J Parris: *Was that in and around the district of Wombwell Main Station near Wood Walk?*
Melling: *Yes.*
Mr E J Parris: *And after you had satisfied yourself you left her to go home?*
Melling: *I didn't like late hours. I had no intention of taking her to her home.*

Having turned to the night of 23 September, Mr Parris asked Melling if, on that night the accused walked past, when he and Mrs Caddick were together. Melling replied:

I saw Caddick following us that night and she saw him too.

Mr E J Parris:	*Notwithstanding that you both carried on with what you were doing, knowing her husband was in the vicinity.*
Melling:	*Yes.*
Mr E J Parris:	*That was the night Mrs Caddick left her home, children and husband.*
Melling:	*Yes, sir.*
Mr E J Parris:	*Do you feel any shame that you broke up this man's home?*
Melling:	*I told her to go home that night.*
Mr E J Parris:	*Yet you continued meeting her and being intimate with her?*
Melling:	*Yes, once or twice a week.*
Mr E J Parris:	*Were you in love with Mrs Caddick?*
Melling:	*I was. I was very reluctant at being intimate with Mrs Caddick on account of my love for her.*
Mr E J Parris;	*And all this is what you referred to as friendship.*
Melling:	*Well, friendship gets from one thing to another.*
Mr E J Parris:	*It is clear to you that she was staying away from home because of you?*
Melling:	*Yes I suppose so.*
Mr E J Parris:	*Did you want her to go back to her husband?*
Melling:	*I told her to go back.*
Mr E J Parris:	*On the Friday night before her death did she tell you she was going back to her husband because she had nowhere to go and that when she found other lodgings she would leave the accused again?*
Melling:	*Yes.*
Mr E J Parris:	*It was all arranged between the two of you. You were party to this sham and pretence!*
Melling;	*Yes.*
Mr E J Parris:	*It was intended that as soon as she obtained fresh lodgings, she would resume her adulterous association with you?*
Melling:	*I suppose so.*

Opening the case for the defence, Mr J E Parris played his trump card when he revealed his surprise witness, Mrs Dale, whom he would call later on in the proceedings. This witness would say that she had seen Mrs Caddick and Melling together at 8.45pm on the night of the incident. He would ask the jury to infer from this that Mrs Caddick had made an assignation for adultery with Melling that very she was with her husband at the hotel. He asked the jury to believe this independent witness rather than the evidence that had been previously given. Later on Mr Parris said, when speaking on a point of law, when a man killed a person it was not necessarily murder because the act could have been committed in self-defence, or as the result of an accident, or as the result of some degree of provocation which deprived that person for the moment of his self control. Mr Parris said the provocation that Caddick had received was such that any reasonable man would lose his self control. Caddick had been subject to acute provocation. Had Caddick committed some violent action on the night when he saw his wife committing adultery with Melling near Wombwell Station, there would not have been the slightest doubt that would have been reasonable provocation. On the night they both knew that Caddick was in the vicinity. Yet they showed a total and utter disregard for all the decencies in life. Mr Parrris then said:

> *While one does not wish to speak disrespectfully of the dead, in this case it must be apparent that Mrs Caddick was an utterly worthless woman ... Caddick had had his wife back and forgiven her, but it was pure sham on her part. She was not the repentant wife and the reconciliation was nothing but a hollow pretence on her part. She only wanted a roof over her head.*

Mr Parris said that the accused did not remember stabbing his wife but he did remember stabbing Melling, and perhaps no one would shed any tears of regret that Melling was injured. Mr Parris further asked if the jury accepted that, if the accused struck the blow after great provocation had destroyed his self-control, they should return a verdict of manslaughter and not murder.

When Alfred Caddick entered the witness block he refused the offer of a chair, and gripping tightly on a handkerchief, which he had in his hand throughout the trial, answered the questions that were put to him in a low voice. Caddick's appearance in the witness bock lasted for an hour. He was handed a wooden model of the dagger exhibit by his defending counsel, Mr Parris. When Mr Parris asked Caddick to demonstrate the trick in which the knife that had been used to stab Mrs Caddick played a part, to the jury, Caddick replied:

If I'm a failure its because I'm very nervous.

His Lordship said although he did not want to stop Caddick from demonstrating the trick it was rather an ordeal for him in such circumstances to be asked to do a conjuring trick in that court. In describing how the trick was done, Caddick said that three pieces of paper were stuck on each side of the blade. Then turning the blade over quickly you took the pieces of paper off in turn. Then magically you put them back on. Mr Parris said:

In fact you have only taken the pieces off one side of the knife and you leave them on the other?

Caddick: *Yes, that's the secret of the trick.*

Replying to a question put to him, by Mr Hylton-Foster, Caddick said he had not used the knife for any conjuring trick on the night of the alleged murder. He had the knife in his pocket for a few days.

In concluding the case for the defence, Mr Parris in his final submission asked the jury to consider that the prosecution had failed to prove their case. Asking them to consider the question of provocation Mr Parris said:

There was never a case where a woman provoked a man more ... Is Melling not the sort of man to snatch a bit of life behind a public house or in any horrible sordid back street? Can you imagine what a contemptuous, humiliating experience it was?

SOUTH YORKSHIRE TIMES AND EXPRESS, MARCH 21st, 1953 9

"NOT GUILTY" OF MURDER

Manslaughter Verdict Against Wombwell Man

Five Years Sentence For Causing Death of His Wife

AFTER a three-day hearing, Alfred Caddick, 46-year-old miner and amateur conjurer, of Foley Avenue, Wombwell, was yesterday found guilty, at Leeds Assize, of the manslaughter of his wife, Edith Caddick (40), and sentenced to five years' imprisonment. Caddick was found not guilty of wilful murder. It was stated that the prisoner had stabbed his wife with a dagger which he had used in a conjuring trick.

The verdict was returned by a jury of ten men and two women, after a retirement lasting 75 minutes.

The case for the defence was conducted by Mr E. J. Parris, assisted by Mr R. C. Hutchinson. (Mr Parris was the barrister in charge of the defence in the recent Craig-Bentley murder trial).

Mr H. B. Hylton-Foster, QC, assisted by Mr C. Aarvold, appeared for the prosecution.

History of "Trouble"

Opening the case for the prosecution, Mr H. B. H. Hylton-Foster, QC, said the Caddick family had consisted of accused, his wife, a married daughter and two sons—Alfred (18) and Douglas (13). For as long as the elder boy remembered there had been "trouble" between the father and the mother. During the past ten years, Mrs Caddick had left home several times but on each occasion had returned. At the latter end of September, she left home for about eight weeks and during that time lived at Hemingfield with a Mr and Mrs Clarke.

She obtained employment with a Chapeltown engineering firm but eventually left and started work at the Milton Arms Hotel, Hemingfield. About August of last year she met Thomas Melling, of Hemingfield, a 34-year-old single miner, and committed adultery with him. On November 15th, Mrs Chaddick returned home to her husband and said Mr Hylton-Foster, "It would seem the accused was glad to have her back." She lived with her husband until November 18th—the day she died.

On that day, accused and Mrs Caddick went to Hemingfield with the intention of collecting Mrs Caddick's belongings from the home of Mr and Mrs Clarke. Later in the evening, accused and his wife had a drink with Mr and Mrs Clarke in the Milton Arms Hotel. About 9.40 p.m., Mrs Caddick said she wished to catch the 10.10 bus to Wombwell and left the hotel.

MRS. CADDICK.

Accused said he would follow on. At 10.5 Mrs Caddick was seen standing alone at the bus stop across from the hotel and shortly after, according to evidence, Melling came up the road. Mrs Caddick called to him and he went across to her.

"Just about that time, accused came out of the hotel and saw his wife with Melling. He rushed across to them," continued Mr Hylton-Foster. Then, according to Melling's evidence, Caddick seized his wife's shoulders, shook her and said, "You are not coming to my —— house tonight!" It was then that Melling was stabbed and he went across to the Milton Arms for assistance.

Accused followed him into the hotel and came out immediately afterwards with Mr Clarke. Seeing Mr Clarke, Mrs Caddick started to run across the road, shouting, "Mr Clarke, Mr Clarke." "As to what happened then, the accounts vary," explained counsel for the prosecution. It would be said that Caddick ran round Mr Clarke, towards his wife, put his arms round her body, "as if to ward her off going in the main door of the hotel." At that time, Mr Clarke received an injury to his hand.

According to a witness, Caddick held a dagger in his hand and struck a blow which appeared to go into his wife's left shoulder. Mr. Clarke went into the hotel and as he passed accused and his wife, heard Caddick say "Oh, what have I done?" or "I've done it now."

Mrs Caddick collapsed and was assisted into the hotel doorway. Soon shortly after Caddick showed distress and remorse and was alleged to have said, "I saw her at the bus stop and he said you can't have her back."

When Mr Hylton-Foster described the stab wound sustained by Mrs Caddick—"five inch in total depth"—the accused bowed his head and wept.

"That is the story of the crime," said the prosecuting counsel. It might be submitted that the accused acted under provocation and there might be an attempt to have the charge reduced from murder to manslaughter.

Mr Hylton-Foster said the dagger used by Caddick was 10 inches long with a 6-inch double-edged blade. "Allowing for the thickness of Mrs Caddick clothes, it might have been plunged up to the hilt," he said.

Son's Evidence

One of the first witnesses to be called was Alfred Caddick, the 18-year-old son of the accused. He told the Court that before the middle of last year, relations between his parents had not been too good. He described one occasion when he saw Melling with his mother and father. His father had stopped him and said: "This is what she is doing." When his father had later asked him what was to be done he had replied: "Don't let her come back into the house!" Being shown the dagger used in the crime, witness said his younger brother had brought it home at the beginning of last year. He last saw it about eight weeks prior to his mother's death. In cross-examination, Caddick said he was fond of his father.

"Has he been as good a father as one could wish?" asked Mr Parris.

"Yes sir!" witness replied.

"Is it fair to say he is a quiet unassuming chap, fond of his family and home life?" continued Mr Parris.

"Yes!" agreed the witness.

Witness then stated that as long as he could remember there had always been trouble at home. His mother used to go away at week-ends without saying where she was going.

"Has she had one man after another, besides your father?" asked Mr Parris.

"I don't know," said Caddick.

In answer to further questions, witness said his mother often became violent and threw things at his father and also struck the accused with her fists.

"And in spite of all that," said Mr Parris, "your father was very much in love with her and was always the first to forgive and make up?" Witness agreed and added that his father was overjoyed when Mrs Caddick returned home the last time.

Found Dagger in Wood

Douglas Caddick, the younger son of the accused, was the next witness to be called and when shown the dagger exhibited in Court said that it belonged to him. He had found it in Wombwell Wood and when at home ad kept it behind a knife box in the kitchen. He last saw it two weeks before his mother's death.

Cross-examined by Mr Parris, witness said his father was quite good at conjuring tricks and although he knew of a trick which was done with a knife had never seen the trick performed. He agreed his father had been good to him and said that his mother left home the last time his father had been ill and off work for some time.

The licensee of the Milton Arms Hotel, Hemingfield, Spencer R. Hazzard said Mrs Caddick had worked at his hotel for a few days a short time before her death. On the night of the incident, he saw Mrs Caddick and her husband in the tap room of the hotel in company with Mr and Mrs Clarke.

"Everybody was quite happy," he said. At 10.25 the same evening, Clarke showed him a knuckle injury and later he saw Melling "who had blood on him." Witness went into the hotel vestibule

ALFRED CADDICK.

where he saw Mrs. Caddick lying on the floor with accused trying to hold her and asking her to speak.

Cross-examined, witness told the court that Mrs Caddick had left his employment because she complained it was "too cold."

"Perhaps you were of the opinion that she was work shy?" asked Mr Parris. After a long pause, witness agreed.

Hazzard said he saw Melling at about 8.45 on the night of the incident. Melling was then in the Hemingfield WMC where witness was playing billiards.

"Very Upset"

Referring to the witness's evidence regarding the accused and his wife when they were seen in the hotel vestibule, Mr Parris asked: "It was probably quite clear to you that the accused was out of his mind?" "He was very upset," replied witness.

Mrs Elsie Clarke, of 20, Quest Avenue, Hemingfield, said that for the six or seven weeks prior to her death, Mrs Chaddick had been lodging at the witness's home. When her son returned home from service in the Forces, witness said that she had to give Mrs Caddick a week's notice as Mrs Caddick was occupying the son's bedroom. On the day of the incident, Mrs Caddick came to the witness's home to collect some clothes and later that evening both witness and her husband had a drink in the Milton Arms with the accused and his wife. Mrs Caddick left the hotel to catch a bus and shortly after witness also left to go home. She did not see Mrs Caddick again.

At the commencement of her cross-examination Mrs Clarke collapsed in the witness-box and had to be assisted out of court.

In view of Mrs Clarke's condition the defence counsel waived his right to cross examination and asked for the next witness to be called.

This was Fred Banhister, of 8, Brown's Square, Hemingfield, who told the court that he was entering the hotel when he saw Mrs Caddick waiting on the opposite side of the road for the Wombwell bus. She was alone. In the hotel he saw Caddick and about 10.15 Caddick left but returned immediately afterwards. He rushed in and shouted to Mr Clarke, "Come here, Bill—quick!"

Shortly after, he saw Mrs Caddick lying in the main passage of the hotel doorway. The accused was kneeling by her side.

Exchanged Greetings

Thomas Melling, who gave his address as 122 Cemetery Road, Hemingfield, was asked what were the relations between himself and Mrs Caddick during the four months that he knew her. Witness replied, "Friendship, sir." On further questioning, he admitted being intimate with Mrs Caddick. He said that the last time he saw her before the night of her death was on the previous Friday. On the night that she died he said that he was walking past the Milton Arms Hotel when he saw Mrs Caddick standing at the bus stop on the opposite side of the road. She shouted him across. They had just exchanged greetings when Caddick came out of the Milton Arms Hotel and rushed across the road — "Like a madman," said witness.

"He shook his wife's shoulders, walked away and then said to his wife, 'You are not coming to my —— house tonight.' He came back and stabbed me," continued Melling.

Cross-examining, Mr Parris said: "One thing is quite clear, Mr Melling — the accused lost control of himself."

"He knew what he was doing," replied witness.

"Are you not thoroughly ashamed of the part you have played in this tragedy?" asked Mr Parris.

"No! I am not," said Melling.

"Is it not clear to you that but for your adultery with this woman she would be alive today?" asked counsel for the defence.

Melling did not reply.

"Not Ashamed"

"You are not ashamed?" said Mr Parris.

"I said I wasn't," replied witness.

Mr Parris went on: "When you met Mrs Cuddick you knew she was married?"

Witness agreed.

"Did you commit adultery with her the first time you met?"

"No, it was three weeks later."

Melling said he first met Mrs Caddick at the Milton Arms. He later made a habit of meeting her in that public house. They used to go into fields during walks.

In reply to Mr Parris, Melling said that when he walked Mrs Caddick home they had intercouse on the way.

"Was that in and around the district of Wombwell Main station near Wood Walk?" asked Mr Parris.

"Yes" said witness.

"And after you had satisfied yourself, you left her to go home?" continued Mr Parris.

"I didn't like late hours," said Melling. "I had no intention of taking her to her home."

"Were you scared of meeting her husband?" queried Mr Parris.

(CONTINUED ON PAGE 16).

South Yorkshire Times

What the accused did that night was reasonable with regard to the provocation he received. He was tortured by the thought and revelation of a plot of complete treacherousness.

Arthur Caddick sobbed throughout Mr Parris's submission.

In concluding the case for the prosecution, Mr Hylton-Foster asked the jury to bear in mind the difference between distinction and duty and reminded them that only one side of the matter had been heard before the court, the deceased woman having no counsel to put her side forward.

Having heard all the evidence in his summing up His Lordship advised the jury:

... You may feel somewhat sympathetic with the accused man because he has had the great misfortune to have an unfaithful wife, but however sympathetic you may feel you should not allow sympathy to conflict with your duty ... The unfaithfulness of a wife affords no justification for an excuse for the husband to stab her to death ... Our law does not permit a man to take the law into his own hands ...

The jury retired and returned with a verdict after seventy-five minutes. The foreman said they found the prisoner not guilty of wilful murder but guilty of manslaughter. His Lordship, addressing Caddick, said:

The jury have brought in a merciful verdict but this is a serious case of manslaughter. I have taken into consideration that the prisoner's wife had been unfaithful and at the time of the incident the prisoner was in poor health caused through his wife having left him. I find that the least sentence consistent with duty is five years' imprisonment.

As the sentence was pronounced Caddick stood pale and motionless in the dock between two warders. During the verdict and sentencing the prisoner's mother-in-law, sister-in-law and other relations were present in Court. Since his wife's death, Caddick had been loyally supported throughout the proceedings that followed by his in-laws, as well as members of his own family.

CHAPTER 15

Polish Lodger Murders his Host's Wife, Springfield Street, Barnsley
June 1953

...as he entered the room, he saw Lubina striking himself in the forehead with some instrument, either scissors or a knife...

On Thursday 25 June 1953, disabled ex-Serviceman and factory hand, Herbert Ball, returned home from work to the sounds of his wife's screams coming from the upper floors of the Springfield Street tenement house, where he and his wife rented a flat on the attic floor from Mr John Varty. Lodging with the Ball's at 15 Springfield Street was forty-two-year-old Polish miner, Wilhelm Lubina. Mr Ball told police later:

When I heard the screaming I spoke to a gentleman who was standing in the doorway and said to him that he could run up the stairs quicker than myself...

The man who ran upstairs was in fact the Ball's landlord, John Varty. When Mr Varty reached the head of the stairs he saw Mrs Ball come from the direction of the living room. Thirty-nine-year-old Charlotte Ball, her clothes stained with blood, was staggering, and Mr Varty could see that blood was streaming from her chest. Mr Varty also saw the Ball's lodger, Wilhelm Lubina, who was striking Mrs Ball with something, in the chest, although exactly what instrument Lubina was using, Mr Varty could not tell. As Mrs Ball came out onto the landing, she fell to the floor, blood was gushing from her wounds. Lubina also fell to the floor, and ended up laying across Charlotte Ball's legs, as he continued to strike blows, which missed their target. When

Lubina saw Mr Varty, he got up and went into the living room. Mr Varty followed him, and as he entered the room he saw Lubina striking himself in the forehead with some instrument, either scissors or a knife, he thought. Blood was pouring down his cheeks and dripping from his chin onto his clothes. Mr Varty closed the door and held it. Shortly afterwards he heard a thud. When he opened the door, Lubina had collapsed on the floor and was unconscious.

Meanwhile, Herbert Ball had climbed the stairs. He said later:

> *I followed the man* [John Varty] *up the stairs and I saw my wife laid at the top of the stairs covered in blood. I could see she was suffering from wounds in the chest.*

Mr Ball said he tried to make his wife as comfortable as possible. He took a vest off Lubina's bed and tried to wipe the blood off his wife's body to see where her injuries were. He stayed with her until the ambulance arrived. Mrs Ball was taken to Beckett Hospital but was found to be dead on arrival. Wilhelm Lubina was also taken to Beckett Hospital.

When police arrived at 15 Springfield Street they found a bloodstained knife in a box on a dresser. Attached to the blood on the knife was a hair, which corresponded to the head hair

Looking towards Barrow Colliery, where Wilhelm Lubina worked. Brian Elliott collection

of Charlotte Ball. From Lubina's belongings in the attic, police took several photographs of Mrs Ball and also a letter, which had been written by Lubina in April, which read:

Dear Lottie,

Your letter arrived on Thursday morning for which I thank you heartily... hope we shall meet each other on Saturday at the normal spot where we go to ...

Yours affectionately,
Willie

An inquest before Deputy West Riding Coroner, S G Beaumont, Esquire, was opened and adjourned the next day. Detective Inspector John Marshall said a man was at present being detained in hospital and would subsequently be charged with causing the death of the woman.

On the day following the attack on Charlotte Ball, her killer was himself responding to treatment, and at 5.30pm was certified to be perfectly rational. Lubina asked to see Detective Inspector Marshall. Detective Inspector James J Marshall, head of Barnsley CID, went to the hospital, where he was told by Lubina that he had killed Mrs Ball and would like to see her body before telling the police anything more about it. The police however were unable to accede to this request and Lubina was neither then, nor at any time later, allowed to see the body. When cautioned, Lubina said that he loved Mrs Ball and had decided to take her life and his own on account of jealousy. Further revelations were made to various police officers during his recovery at Beckett Hospital. Detective Constable Arthur Carr was later to give evidence during the committal proceedings in which he stated shortly after being visited by a priest, under caution, Lubina said:

Father wants to know about my health. He gave me communion. I tell him that English father see me this morning. You will know I make big mistake. I save plenty trouble to police and others. Doctor say I just missed heart with that much.

DC Carr said that Lubina then indicated with his fingers that he meant about an inch. On the evening of 28 June DC Carr was again at Lubina's bedside, when Lubina said to him:

> *You will know man can have a friend. A woman can have a husband and one friend but not a husband and many friends.*

Lubina said Mrs Ball had told him she had a male acquaintance in Newcastle and she had shown him a photograph of the man. She also had said she had met a man in Leeds, although she had told her husband she had gone to Leeds to see a female friend. Lubina went on to say that he lived with Charlie and Lottie (Mrs and Mrs Ball) and helped them because Charlie was an invalid and because he felt sorry for them, before adding:

> *I no care, I want no defence. I kill her. I kill her. If I hang – no matter. I hang. I told Polish Major I want no help, my life is finished. I do not wish for defence. I tell you that I keep my secret. Better we both die, she now die and I live only a little longer.*

A present-day view of Springfield Street (No. 15 is on the right). The author.

On 3 July, Lubina said that earlier in the week before Charlotte Ball's death, Herbert Ball had opened a letter from the man at Newcastle, before his wife had seen it and had broken down in tears. Feeling uncomfortable about this, Lubina went on to say he had told Mr Ball that he would leave the house on Friday but Mr Ball had told Lubina to stay. It emerged that Lubina earned good wages, £15 or £16 each week and would spend £6 or £7 a week on the three of them. Lubina said:

> *We are very good friends. If I spend lots of money he must understand. I love her very much. Why, why does she lie so much? I give my last shirt to her!*

On Thursday 23 July Lubina appeared before Barnsley magistrates for committal proceedings. He was conveyed to the court by ambulance. Surprisingly, there were no spectators outside the court, as the ambulance drew up to within just a few feet of the doorway. Lubina wore a grey suit and an American-style check shirt. In making a remand in custody for one week Police Superintendent Legg said that the papers in the case were being sent to the Director of Public Prosecutions. Speaking on behalf of the defendant, Mr S Temple-Milnes of Bradford, said he had no objection to the application. The chairman, Mrs E Allum, in remanding Lubina to HM Prison at Leeds, said that legal aid would be granted. In the proceedings that followed full details of the case became known. The revelations made by Lubina during his hospitalisation were described by Mr Temple-Milnes as being a policeman's paradise and the sort of thing a policeman dreams about, to be told such information without asking questions.

The widower of the victim, Mr Herbert Ball, entered the courtroom with the assistance of a walking stick. During his evidence Mr Ball said, in January 1948, he and his wife made the acquaintance of Lubina, while they were at an inn at Dodworth. Charlotte Ball was German-born. They heard Lubina speaking in a foreign tongue and quite an argument ensued between husband and wife as to what nationality the man was. This resulted in them approaching Lubina to satisfy their curiosity. Lubina was able to understand and speak German better than English and so by conversing in both languages, the Balls struck up a friendship with Lubina, who worked at Barrow Colliery and was then living at the *Miners' Hotel*, Barnsley. When Lubina's English failed him Charlotte Ball was able to converse with him in German and a strong friendship grew between the three of them, resulting in, on 2 May 1953, Lubina coming to live with the Balls at Springfield Street. They had taken him in because he had always been good to them and they had told him if they got anywhere in life they would take him with them. When asked if he had ever had any suspicions that there was something going on between Lubina and his wife, Mr Ball said that he had once, about twelve months previously. He asked his wife to meet him at an inn. She had earlier gone to another inn with a friend. Mr Ball said:

> *I kept my appointment but Mrs Ball did not. I waited about ten minutes and then went to the other inn, where I saw Lubina and my wife, they were together. She said that she was talking to someone on business. I got a bit riled and she said she did not want that type. She was referring to Lubina.*

Mr Ball then went on to describe the events on the day of his wife's death.

Police Constable Stevens said that when he went to the house he saw Mrs Ball lying at the top of the stairs. An examination revealed five stab wounds above her right breast and one on her left breast. Her outstretched arms and legs were also covered in blood and a large pool of blood was on the floor. She was wearing a yellow jumper and a red and white leaf pattern skirt.

Mrs Evelyn Leader, who lived in a room on the first floor of the house, said, on 25 June, she heard noises coming from the attic. She heard furniture being moved followed by screams from Mrs Ball. She heard Lubina speaking in his own language. It sounded as though they were fighting and the commotion continued for about fifteen minutes.

Dr Magri, of the Beckett Hospital, said when he had made a thorough examination of the whole of Lubina's body, he found only the wounds about the head and chest, which appeared to be stab wounds, but he did not know. These wounds were not particularly deep and appeared to have been self-inflicted.

Dr David E Price, consultant and Home Office pathologist, attached to the North Eastern Forensic Science Laboratory at Wakefield, described Mrs Bell's wounds, which he said fell into three categories. Dr Price said the first group of wounds could have been produced by an instrument about one inch across by four inches long, an instrument consistent with the knife produced in court. The first wound was into the upper and outer corner of the right breast. This wound had been produced when the instrument went in at the armpit and finished at the third rib, which had been fractured on impact. The second wound was into the upper and outer corner of the left breast and went obliquely inwards through the second rib into the left lung.

The next group of wounds, of which there were four, were on the right side of the front of the chest, sited close to the breastbone. The first wound penetrated the chest wall and went through the lung to its root. The second penetrated the chest wall but did not injure the lung. The third wound ran obliquely downwards through the skin of the chest wall. The last wound ran obliquely in through the chest wall downwards and to the left to penetrate the wall of the heart. There were two small holes in the main artery just above the heart, probably caused by the heart bumping across the end of the knife. On the left side of the chest wall there was a small nick in the skin with a scratch below it.

The third group of wounds consisted of scratches on the right forearm just above the thumb and on the left upper arm just above the elbow. There was a slight bruising to the right wrist and left hand. These could have been defence wounds, they were trivial and confined to the skin. Cause of death was shock and haemorrhage, following stab wounds to the chest.

Dr F G Trihorn, Director of the North Eastern Forensic Science Laboratory, gave evidence concerning several exhibits including the knife used to stab Mrs Ball and several items of clothing. The knife was made entirely of metal, with the handle painted bottle red. The blade was four inches long and tapered from its greatest width of ¾ in. to a sharp point. There were heavy bloodstains along the full length of the blade which appeared to have been recently sharpened. Dr Trihorn said he found on the knife's handle a single human hair which was found to agree in all characters with a sample of head hair from the dead woman.

Wilhelm Lubina was committed for trial to Leeds Assizes on charges of murder and attempting to commit suicide. On Saturday 5 December 1953 the *Barnsley Chronicle* reported that week's proceedings at Leeds Assizes. Mr H B H Hylton Foster, QC, prosecuting, said that Lubina had told the police that he loved the woman and jealousy caused him to attack her. Lubina had tried to commit suicide after he had attacked the woman. He had seven stab wounds in his right temple and three in his chest.

From the dock Lubina, with tears streaming down his face, called out in Polish:

> *… I am sorry … I am not punishable … I lost control … I lost my consciousness …*

Speaking through an interpreter, Lubina described how he returned from work to the house in Springfield Street. He said that Mrs Ball was in her room. He entered the room and washed his hands and she gave him some bread and cheese. He read the newspaper and, when he had done so, he told her he was leaving the next day. She said she was waiting for this moment and then she lost her temper and hit him with her fists and she shouted:

> *Swine. Go away from me you swine. I asked what she hit me for and she then kicked me. She hurt me and I lost my head. Then as I jumped up from the floor where she knocked me, I grabbed something on the table. I hit her. I lost my control and don't remember how many times I hit her.*

Lubina said that Mrs Ball, about a fortnight previously, after having attacked him, had given him her assurance that she would not hit him again:

I told her I had never hit a woman before and didn't want a woman to hit me … I lost my head then …

Defending, Mr J Basil Herbert, said, it was now known that what Lubina had picked up was in fact a knife. Lubina agreed that this was the case, but he did not know where a knife was, he did not put the knife on the table, then added:

I hit her and lost my control. I hit her a few times. I don't remember how many times – I heard from a doctor in the court at Barnsley, six times…I am very sorry for what I have done and I am very sorry that through her I am accused of murder.

Mr Herbert asked:

Did you hate this woman?

To which Lubina replied with great vehemence:

Never!

Then Mr Herbert asked Lubina:

Did you at any time in your right mind want to kill her?

Again came the answer:

Never!

Mr Herbert asked Lubina why when he regained consciousness in hospital with knife wounds alleged to have been self-inflicted, he asked to see Mrs Ball. Lubina replied that he could not believe that he had killed her. He said on recovering consciousness, there was a newspaper lying on the bed and he saw his name on it and read of the tragic day in which he was involved.

The jury, having considered their verdict, found Wilhelm Lubina guilty of wilful murder. The clerk of arraigns asked Lubina if he had anything to say before sentence was passed, to which came his barely audible, mumbled reply:

I did not wish to kill her.

Lubina remained unmoved as Mr Justice Stable passed the death sentence on him. The execution was provisionally scheduled for 16 December. His appeal having been dismissed, Wilhelm Lubina, then aged forty-three, was executed at Armley Gaol on 25 January 1953. Following an inquest, held later that morning, Lubina's body was buried within Armley's precincts.

Sources and Further Reading

Chapter 1

The Barnsley Times, March 28 1857; January 16, February 27 1858; January 29 1859; April 6, 13, 20 1861; April 5, July 19 1862; May 16 1863; August 13 1864; January 28, August 19 1865; August 18 1866; April 6, December 14 1867; January 18 1868; March 25, April 1 1871.

The Barnsley Chronicle And Penistone, Mexbro', Wath, And Hoyland Journal, December 14, 28 1867; August 29 1868; June 7 1879.

The Sheffield And Rotherham Independent, June 4 1879; August 24 1893.

The Sheffield Daily Telegraph, June 4 1879.

The Barnsley Independent, March 1 1884; July 30 1892; March 4 1893; March 23 1901.

Chapter 2

The Times, April 8, September 1 1901.

The Barnsley Independent, February 9, March 23 1901; January 28 1905; May 9 1908.

The Barnsley Chronicle And Penistone, Mexbro', Wath, And Hoyland Journal, November 8 1902; November 7 1903.

Chapter 3

The Barnsley Independent, June 29, September 7 1912; June 7 1919; January 10, May 8 1920; August 25, September 1, December 8 1923; February 21 1925.

The Barnsley Standard, Saturday June 29 1912.

Chapter 4

The Barnsley Chronicle & South Yorkshire News, January 14 1933; January 1 1938; July 30 1938; January 5, April 13 1946; May 24, September 6, 27 1947; April 10 1948; January 7, April 22 1950; December 20 1952.

Chapter 5

The Barnsley Chronicle And Penistone, Mexbro', Wath, And Hoyland Journal, November 15 1902.

The Barnsley Chronicle And South Yorkshire News, June 28 1930; March 18 1933.

The Barnsley Times, February 27 1858; August 19 1865; August 15 1868; March 1 1884.

The Sheffield And Rotherham Independent, August 24 1893.

The Barnsley Independent, October 13 1883; May 9 1908; January 22 1916; November 10, December 15 1923.

Chapter 6

The Barnsley Times, March 21, 28 1857; May 3, July 19 1862; August 19 1865; July 10 1875.

The Sheffield And Rotherham Independent, November 12 1892.

The Barnsley Chronicle And Penistone, Mexbro', Wath And Hoyland Journal, May 3, July 19 1862.

The Barnsley Chronicle & South Yorkshire News, February 28, 1953.

The Barnsley Independent, March 23 1901; January 22 1916; May 8 1920; March 3 1923.

Chapter 7

The Sheffield And Rotherham Independent, November 4 1892.

Barnsley Chronicle, May 17, July 5 1930.

Barnsley Chronicle And South Yorkshire News, July 29 1930; September 27 1947; September 6 1956.

Barnsley Independent, May 21 1892; August 1 1903; October 19 1912; January 20 1923.

South Yorkshire Times & Express, July 11 1953.

Chapter 8

The Barnsley Times And General Advertiser, And Record of Mining And Manufacturing Interests, July 28, December 22 1860.

The Barnsley Chronicle And Penistone, Mexbro', Wath, And Hoyland Journal, July 28 1860.

Chapter 9

The Barnsley Times And General Advertiser, And Record of Mining And Manufacturing Interests, April 11, August 15 1868.

The Barnsley Chronicle And Penistone, Mexbro', Wath, And Hoyland Journal, April 11, August 15 1868.

Chapter 10
The Barnsley Chronicle And Penistone, Mexborough, Wath And Hoyland Journal, October 10, 17 1868.
The Barnsley Times, October 10, 17 1868.

Chapter 11
The Barnsley Independent, June 13, 20, August 8, 15, 22, December 12 1919.
The Barnsley Chronicle, 5 December 1903.

Chapter 12
Barnsley Chronicle And Penistone, Mexbro', Wath And Hoyland Journal, October 31, November 7, December 3, 12 1903.

Chapter 13
The Times, June 11 1948.
The Barnsley Chronicle And South Yorkshire News, March 6, April 10, May 8 1948

Chapter 14
South Yorkshire Times And Express, November 20 1952, January 17, March 21 1953.
Barnsley Chronicle & South Yorkshire News, November 22, 29, December 20 1952; January 17, March 21 1953.

Chapter 15
Barnsley Chronicle & South Yorkshire News, June 25, July 25, August 1, December 5 1953.
The Times, January 12 1954.

Index